More Than a Country Song

My Story. Our connection. A road map to living your authentic purpose.

JONELLE MARIE CARTER

More than a Country Song
Copyright © 2020 by Jonelle Marie Carter
All rights reserved.
First Edition: 2020

Photography by Jacquelyne Rochelle Johnson
Facebook @jacquelynerochellejohnson
Cover and Formatting: Streetlight Graphics

No part of this book may be reproduced, scanned, or distributed in any printed or electronic form without permission. Please do not participate in or encourage piracy of copyrighted materials in violation of the author's rights. Thank you for respecting the hard work of this author.

Dedication

For Megha who raises me up, trail-blazes a path with her elegance and fearlessness and gives back to mankind with compassion and tender generosity. Our friendship has withstood the test of time, distance and hurdles. Despite being raised in different cultures, countries and times we are yet sisters. This dedication is for you...for believing in me endlessly and for your ability to see everything that I could be long before I ever could.

For Erin-

Friendship chose us long before we were ever aware. There are not enough pages to fully depict the deep rooted connection that has anchored us together. Thank you for the years of advice, daily talks, guidance and sisterhood that has led me to the path I am on today. I can't wait to watch the flamingos and listen to the waves crash while we grow into crazy old ladies together.

For T-

There was no music
until I heard your name....

Intro

"Raise your hand if you feel like you have lived multiple lifetimes within one lifetime…"

This is the first line I wrote for a presentation I gave in October 2019 to a group of amazing women in Ohio. I'm a singer and songwriter, not a speaker, but I was so flattered to have been asked to be the keynote speaker for a women's professional empowerment event called "The Power Of Her" that I accepted the invitation immediately.

So after saying my opening statement out loud, I actually raised my own hand and then laughed at myself. Mainly because I am a huge dork, but also because it never ceases to amaze me how much I still learn from myself.

Today I went to the gym to meet my trainer, Ro, my new best friend and the person who believes in me when I want to give up. Or more specifically, the person I can trust not to call an ambulance when I truly think I am dying because she knows I am, in fact, not dying. Also, Ro doesn't realize that she is my new best friend, but anyone who is willing to hug me when I am sweating from my inner elbows is a best friend in my eyes.

As I was walking into the Y to meet Ro, I realized I was giving myself a pep talk: "Everything is going to be okay. You have a lot to say and someone…someone will listen. They will hear you. Just be you. Stop second guessing yourself and trust the journey." You see, the previous night I had a dream that I was speaking at a different event somewhere outdoors and full of college kids, and everyone was ignoring me and talking over the speakers so loudly that I couldn't hear myself. I had a really good point to get across, but no one could hear me, and I woke up in a panic trying to remember what the point was. What was it that was *so* important that I ended up telling the crowd off? If you know me, and you will get to, then you know that this is *not* something that I would normally do. I run from any kind of confrontation, conflict, face-offs, or battles. I am not the friend you want to back you in a bar fight. Ask my friend Jodie, who knows when to tell me it's safe to get out of the car after a road rage situation comes to a head. Who was backing her? I am shamefully not raising my hand for that one.

Don't judge, it had nothing to do with her. I'm afraid of a lot of things, like drinks from strangers and unidentified rashes. Random, I know, but the one common thread is that I'm sure that all of these things will somehow kill me. Just like the elliptical that Ro puts me on. I know it's cliché to stick in the phrase "what doesn't kill you makes you stronger" right here, but there's no better way to say it. And it's really true. All of the painful experiences we go through in our lifetime are how we grow, transition, and become a stronger version of who we were yesterday. Without fear, without conflict, without the elliptical, we stay exactly the same, and that doesn't work well in a world that is constantly moving and changing.

As we grow and raise ourselves up, we enter new phases of our lives, new journeys, and new transitions. Like the ocean with wave after wave changing the ocean floor below, we too are constantly in a state of change. When I am speaking with someone about changes in their life or when a friend or client comes to me for advice, I try to convey this concept. When something feels really awful, I ask them to feel the emotion, and then take a good look inside at what the lesson could be. Some lessons are clear as day, some take years or a lifetime to understand. I have lessons that I have learned and put away, lessons that I am learning right now, and lessons to come.

My sincere hope with this book is that I am able to help someone through a lesson that I have already learned. That you all can help me through the lessons that I am knee deep in now, and that together we can move arm in arm into the next journey and the next set of lessons to come. While reading this book I will hold you up, you will hold me up, and when you're done reading the last chapter, page, and word, we will have formed a new bond, a new friendship that will hold us both up.

Chapter One
This Town

I CAN TRUTHFULLY SAY THAT I grew up with gunshots ringing right in my backyard. But not how you think…

My dad built the house where I grew up in 1975 in a tiny river town sixty miles southwest of Chicago. It was a simple ranch home with white siding and shutters on a sleepy road centered between the Illinois River, the hunt club, and the railroad tracks. Sometimes at night you could hear the barges chugging down the river, sometimes a slow-moving train full of grain and other freight being moved through the Midwestern nights. On brisk fall days you could hear the explosion of gunfire coming from the hunt club. At the time, it didn't make us stop in our tracks. We just knew that if we heard the gunshots, it meant it was fall.

Every time it rained, the front yard would flood, and water would rise up over the green grass so that it peeked out like the little Play-Doh hair that you could push out of the hair-cutting kit. Sometimes the water would freeze and we would have our very own personal ice-skating rink. But most of the time it was just warm enough to create a little pond in the front yard. I used to pretend we were lakeside and staying at a fancy resort with a water feature. My dad, on the other hand, would lose sleep pumping out the water across the road. Not much of a resort for him.

Our living room was sunny and welcoming and boasted a large picture window with thick, heavy drapes made of a rough material that felt scratchy. If these drapes had a personality, I imagined they would be very serious and somewhat crabby. On the right side of the window hung a strong cord that would pull the draperies back and reveal a bright and warm front yard, sometimes complete with… yep, you guessed it—a pond.

So what do window treatments have to do with the topic of life? This window and these drapes played a big role in who I became later in life. You see, these drapes were the first stage curtains I knew. There was music playing constantly in our home. My dad had a nice record player, CD player, and radio hooked into speakers that looked like two sugar cubes stacked on top of each other. The speakers hung from the corners of the living room. Later when my parents put the back addition onto our house, my dad added another set of speakers identical to the living room pair. You could toggle between the two sets or turn all of them on, turning our entire house into a giant speaker.

On winter weekends and lazy summer days my little brother, Chris, would play stagehand as I counted down to the opening of my first show. Flashlight-microphone in hand, we would count *five, four, three, two, annnnd…one!*

Showtime! Chris would crank back the curtains and reveal my stage. My audience of birds and cars passing by was transformed into an audience full of people swaying arm in arm to the music against the night sky. As I finished the last choreographed number, I could hear the crowd cheer as I took one final bow before stagehand Chris would then pull on the cord and close up shop. Sometimes I would be ready for a second show, but Chris usually lost interest by then and moved on to something else.

Our neighborhood was full of kids, mostly boys and a few girls. We played games like kick the can, football, freeze tag, PIG, and steal the bacon. But the ultimate Union Street thing to do was to find fool's gold. The alley that ran between the Union Street houses and the Lincoln Street houses was chock full of fool's gold, and we would fill up our buckets and trade our bigger hunks for things like pieces of gum or sherbet Push-Ups. Some days I wish I had a pocket full of fool's gold…or at least a Push-Up.

Being raised in a small town meant that you were friends with the other village kids from kindergarten to forever. I was lucky to have had a very special class of friends who are still close today. We have done it all together—growing up, love, loss, all of it. The kids who went to school together were the same kids who were at church, camp, the pool, the playground, high school dances, football games, graduation parties, weddings, graduation parties of *their* kids, and on and on.

In fifth grade we decided to put together a band. I was *so* excited because I already had years of stage (*ahem*, window) experience and was sure I would get the roll of lead singer. Much to my disappointment I ended up being the keyboard player. I guess it made me well rounded. (Shout out to all of my amazing piano players over the years. Be glad it's you and not me.)

In grade school, everyone was required to go to music class. This was by far the best class of the day for me. We got to play wooden percussion instruments and make funny noises with our mouths. We learned songs about pumpkins rolling off of fences and silly songs about wanting nothing but our two front teeth for Christmas. Around the same time that my friends and I started our "band", Mrs. Graham, our music teacher, introduced us to Solo and Ensemble. We would pick a piece of music to perform as a solo, duo, or trio act and go to other schools to sing our songs in front of judges who would give us scores and critique our performances. Other than my home-based stage, this was my first taste of performing. It is really interesting to me how early these seeds were planted. My love of performing started at a young age, and I had no idea then how many hours of my life I would spend performing.

Along with music my number one most favorite thing to do was write poetry. I would close the door to my bedroom and sit in deep thought. I would emerge hours later with a piece of paper and a proudly puffed chest. I can remember the way it physically felt to put rhyming words together that described how I was feeling. I would run to my parents and proudly read my poems. Most of them back in the day went something like this: "Snow is white, snow is cold. It is not something you can hold. I love snow and snow loves me. I am glad that snow is free."

Hey, everyone has to start somewhere.

When I was twelve I won a poetry contest, and I got to

go to a school event called "Meet The Author". The authors sat at big, long brown tables and signed their books for us kids. When it was my turn to step up to the table, I was shaking with nerves. I clutched the piece of paper with my poem printed on it in my sweaty little fist. The author reached his hand across the table and gently motioned for me to give it to him. He was a small man with gray, wiry hair and a short gray scruffy beard. He was wearing a red flannel shirt and suspenders and reminded me of someone who might live in Minnesota in the woods.

His face was blank as he scanned the paper, and finally, after what seemed like a lifetime, a smile slowly crept across his weathered face and he told me that he did, in fact, like it. This was the start of my love of writing. Not every critique has been so gentle, but nevertheless here I am. Still writing.

I would like to consider my family quite normal. I grew up with a very small immediate family and a lot of extended family around. My parents are still married and live in the house I grew up in. We still call the middle bedroom "my bedroom", and you can still find boxes of pictures stuck in the front bedroom, more commonly known as "Chris's room".

My mom was born in France to a French mother and an Italian-Irish father who was living in France on an airbase but who had grown up in America. My mother was born in and lived in France until my grandparents moved her to America when she was just a young child. My grandparents (Memere and Pepere, French slang for Grandma and Grandpa) were seriously the coolest. Memere drove a red convertible and cooked things like escargot and handmade spinach ravioli. She was trained by French chefs in her younger years and instilled a love of cooking in all of the women in my family. I could write an entire chapter on her recipes alone. My Pepere was larger than life. Jet-black hair and blue eyes. He was a well-respected nuclear waste engineer and traveled the country speaking about that subject. He was always ready for a good time. He liked martinis and red wine, and he loved when family and friends would come over and have an impromptu dinner. He loved dropping by just to say "hello darlin'" and maybe giving us a mason jar of antipasto, or boozy dark-red cherries that he would soak for weeks before cracking them open for everyone to taste. He built homes and bought land and made friends everywhere he went. When he was building his last home, he pulled a nail out of a stud, stuck it in a wine cork, and handed it to me. He told me to use that nail to build my first home. He pulled quarters out of our ears and had two-dollar bills in his wallet at all times. After he passed away we started finding quarters in the strangest places. They even fall out of thin air, but that was my Pepere—always up for a surprise.

My father was born in the Midwest. His parents, my other set of grandparents, were much older than my maternal grandparents. My grandmother was raised on fertile Midwestern farmland and visited Chicago in the summer to see family. She went on to college and became a teacher. She taught in a one-room schoolhouse and then eventually a full school. She sewed and always had homemade chocolate chip cookies in a glass cookie jar and tart lemonade in her fridge.

My father's father, my other grandpa, Rex Fish, was a

God-loving, faithful churchgoing man. He worked for Caterpillar until his retirement. He built things like wooden cars and crayon caddies in their root cellar-type basement. He died when I was just fourteen, but I have vivid memories of him teaching me how to play card games and singing songs from the forties to me.

Grandpa was white-haired by the time I was born and combed his hair straight over and sprayed it with a squirt of strong men's hairspray. He and my grandma would play cards after every meal. They studied the Bible together, had weekly prayer groups at their home, and served as greeters at church every Sunday that I can remember.

They lived in a large yellow house on the main street in town. It was over one hundred years old with a slamming screen door and porches on three sides. My father kept a large garden at my grandparents' house, and we would bring baskets of rhubarb up the hill and my grandmother would cut them up and simmer them with sugar to cut the tartness. We would pile it high on top of vanilla ice cream and sit in the golden summer sun together and watch the birds fly by.

In the front of their yard sat two of the largest buckeye trees you have ever seen. Every fall, the buckeye casings would fall to the ground and break open, revealing the shiny brown buckeye seeds. Kids from school would walk past the yard and collect buckeyes, stuffing their pockets full. My grandparents' home became known as "the buckeye house". To this day we continue to keep buckeyes as a good luck charm.

This was a place of peace for me. I still feel a twinge of pain when I drive by and see the house that was ours. I hope whoever lives there now can feel the love seeping from the walls, because believe me, there was plenty.

Growing up, we took on a lot of my European-influenced mother's roots, and in a home set in the middle of small town USA, that was…well…interesting. My favorite foods were things like escargot and bagna cauda (Italian hot dip made with garlic and anchovies). We ate fish, lemons, and vinaigrette. We had baguette instead of Wonder Bread, and thin-sliced salami and Italian ham instead of Oscar Mayer. We didn't know any differently until we started school. The other day over a wine tasting, my dear friend Sara recalled the time I cried because the school gave us a stick of yellow government cheese with our chili at lunch, and the lunch lady made me finish it. So started my hate of cheese until recently, when I discovered how well cheese and wine go together. Wine really makes everything better. Kidding, not kidding.

My husband thinks it's funny when I tell him the story about the first time I had SpaghettiOs. I spent the night at a friend's house and her parents were both at work. I didn't have very much time alone without parents at my house, so this felt pretty adult-like and really cool. We were hungry and she was in charge of feeding her little brother. She spun the lazy Susan and pulled out a can of SpaghettiOs with meatballs, dumped them into a scratched-up yellow Tupperware bowl, and stuck it in the microwave.

The orange tomato sauce stuck to the sides of the bowl, melting the burned tomato and yellow plastic together in a clump. My friend pulled out two forks and handed me one. I stuck the fork into a meatball, but it didn't fall apart like the meatballs I was used to. I popped the hot meatball dripping in orange stuff in my mouth and slowly chewed it up and swallowed hard. It didn't taste like anything I had tasted before and it made my stomach flip-flop. It was the first—and last—time I had pasta from a can.

Please don't think that this means I was raised privileged. It also doesn't mean that I was raised less fortunate. There were many times that we would eat whatever came out of the garden and have vegetarian-style meals on hot summer days. We were simply different, something I learned to embrace early on in life.

By this point in the book, you're probably wondering why you need to know so much about my family and what we ate for dinner. I mean, who really cares, right? Well, I thought long and hard about how I was going to explain what happened next. You see, it's one of the number one lessons I hope to get across to you. One of the most important parts of this journey. I feel that society teaches us that people who struggle come from struggle. People who are alcoholics come from a long line of alcoholics, people who are abused watched generations before them live through abuse.

When I was born, I was set down upon such a strong foundation for success that nothing should have been able to penetrate or weaken it. The brackets, the concrete, the stability of this platform that I stood on should have been guaranteed for life. But when I turned fourteen, everything crumbled.

Chapter Two
The Island Song

I was a sick kid. Every October I would get croup and end up in the hospital. This made for a lot of really bad Halloweens. My mom would do her best to make me feel like I was still going to be part of the festivities by dressing me up as an old lady with white-colored hair spray and a shawl to keep me warm. She would let me sit by the door and hand out candy to the other kids.

My oldest friend, Erin, had the best costumes in town. Her mom was an interior designer and had the ability to recover furniture and sew things like costumes. Every year the hardware store in town had a costume parade with free hot dogs. Erin won the costume contest every year. Her best costume to date? I'm voting for the Statue of Liberty.

I was tall for my age and lanky. All arms and legs. I would have made a really funny-looking Statue of Liberty, but Erin wore it perfectly. She had straw-blonde hair that turned white in the summer, sky-blue eyes, and red cheeks, with a giggle that was so infectious it could make the devil himself happy.

Around this same time, our parents let us go trick or treating by ourselves. We would only go down the street, and there was always a squad car patrolling, so it was a pretty safe adventure. One exceptionally dark and cold Halloween, we marched down the broken sidewalk that ran from my driveway all the way to the end of the block. I knew every crack, ledge, and curve of this sidewalk, so walking at night wasn't a challenge. Each step brought the crunch of fallen leaves from large oak trees that grew tall in the yards.

There was something creepy in the air this particular night. We held on tight to our makeshift candy bags made from old pillowcases and rang each doorbell along the way. About halfway down the block, the air became thick and the streetlights seemed dimmer. A truck, owned by a neighbor, was pulled slightly onto the sidewalk, so we had to walk around it. As we came around the back side of the truck, we realized we were alone. We had lost the slew of other neighbor kids and friends along the way, and it suddenly became apparent how dark the night had become. Erin gripped my arm tightly and let me lead her around the rusty truck. Just as we stepped back onto the sidewalk, a large man came running from the house with flailing arms, growling and hairy. Erin screamed as we stood in the middle of the sidewalk, frozen and unable to move. It took us both a few seconds to realize we were standing face to face with a giant gorilla. All at once, the gorilla, who we were sure was trying to kill us, walked slowly back to his house, shaking his head and laughing. A harmless prank by a neighbor.

Erin and I never went trick or treating again. In some ways this was the end of an era. Not long after this I would end up having the first of many surgeries throughout my early teen years. That Halloween seemed like the last bit of my childhood.

At fourteen my mom and I were heading home from a shopping trip. I had been experiencing dull pain in my right lower side for a few days, and with every bump we hit on the ride home, I cringed a little more. We went home and unloaded the car. I decided to try lying on my bed with my butt in the air in hopes that the nagging, pulling pain would somehow magically disappear. No luck. By midnight I was writhing in pain, so my mom drove me to the hospital. There, they quickly did an evaluation and ordered blood work and an ultrasound.

Being that I was fourteen, I had never been to a gynecologist. My first experience with a pelvic exam was under bright white lights in the emergency department. The doctor told my mom that the ultrasound showed a large ovarian cyst about the size of a small grapefruit. Before discharging me, they gave me a shot of Demerol that was big enough to knock out a horse. My dad had to carry me from the driveway to my bed in the middle of the night when we got home.

The next day we had a follow-up visit that included a lot of chaos and an emergency surgery. While the surgeon was removing the cyst, he noted that I had a large amount of abnormal tissue throughout my entire abdomen. He delivered the news to my parents that I would have fertility issues if and when I decided to start a family. I recovered pretty quickly from the surgery but was left shaken, a little more mature, and feeling a little different than my other friends who were still trading Laffy Taffys for Gobstoppers.

This was the beginning of years of lower abdominal pain, mystery symptoms, and exploratory surgeries. During one particular surgery they removed my gallbladder and appendix thinking those might be causing the problem, another time they removed more cysts and scar tissue caused by the endometriosis, and yet another time they went in just to look and see how bad things had become.

I began a series of injections that would basically take me through early menopause and then in reverse in the hope of delaying anymore abnormal tissue from forming outside of my uterus. I learned words like adhesions, Versed, and anesthesiology. I knew how to do things like cough into a spirometer to make sure my lungs stayed clear, shower without getting Steri-Strips wet, and hold my breath while staples were pulled from my now scarred abdomen. Most of my friends were learning high school math and playing sports while I was perfecting the pillow-in-the-stomach-when-you-need-to-cough move.

Around the same time I had my first surgery, I met two men who would equally affect my life in ways that would change me forever, but at this time they weren't men, just boys. Each played a role so significant in my world and yet so opposite of each other that it's hard to believe, even now, that I'm still affected by them today. Both of these boys were excellent students, excellent athletes, and had bright futures ahead of them. Both went off to college and earned degrees. Both have sustainable careers and enough money to retire comfortably. Let's call them Ed and Steve.

It was 1993 and Ed was supposed to take me to the Valentine's dance, but he was an aspiring athlete and had an opportunity to travel out of state to further his chances of becoming something really big in the sport. Steve stepped in during third period typing class and asked me to go with him. Spoiler alert: I ended up dating Steve until I was twenty-one, and as I type this, our son who we had together when I was twenty is going to be twenty-one in a few months. It almost sounds like a math word problem, my least favorite part of my least favorite subject in school. Steve was really great at math and made sure to tell me every chance he got how smart he was. I was not so great at math, and Steve made sure to tell me every chance he got how dumb that made me.

Steve was a bad boy. Not a motorcycle-riding, skipping-school bad boy. He was good at school and grew up on a farm where he did things like participating in 4-H and detasseling corn. Steve was more of a bad boy in the style of calling girls "woman" and not calling you back for days on end, not putting in much effort at all, really. Which made me a bad boy chaser.

Ed, on the other hand, was a complete gentleman. He moved from Texas to our school during his junior year, and all the girls swooned over the way he held the door for us and how he said "y'all" and "ma'am". I was a freshman and Ed was a senior, but that didn't stop us from becoming fast friends.

I was tall for my age and well developed, so I looked eighteen when I was fourteen. Because of this I got a lot of attention from boys, and in turn, it made me boy crazy. I was not shy or afraid to talk to a boy when I entered high school, so I looked up Ed's phone number in the phone book and gave him a call to introduce myself. Word spread fast, and the senior cheerleaders liked to make fun of me by asking me if I had a crush on "Tex", the nickname given to him by the guys. Regardless, Ed never thought twice about walking me down the hall to class or saying hi during lunch. What he didn't realize then was that he was setting a standard for the way I should have been treated in relationships. But by the time he came home from his trip that February, the Valentine's dance had come and gone, and Steve had swept me off of my feet…actually, it was more like he just assumed I was going to be his girlfriend, and that was that. I was the swooning underclassman and he was the starting football player. Sounds like a pretty decent start, right?

Ed and Steve both graduated in May of 1993. Ed moved back down South to go to college, and Steve moved south too but stayed in Illinois. Just like that both boys were gone.

I continued a long-distance relationship with Steve, which in hindsight was just plain crazy. For both of us. Instead of going to dances and hanging with my high school friends, I was lying awake at night worrying about where Steve was or what he was doing, and instead of focusing on college classes, Steve was coming back home to take me to prom. It was never a healthy relationship by any stretch of the imagination, but I was already thinking thoughts like, "He doesn't care if you stay or go. He can do better, so you'd better stay because he's really smart, successful, and hard to get a hold of. You should be really proud that you're a sophomore in high school but your boyfriend is in college. That makes you something, right?" So I stayed in it, convinced that I would never find anyone else to like me.

By the time the end of the year came along, Steve had successfully turned his 4.0 in academics into a 4.0 in keg stands and shotgunning Old Milwaukee. The once completely focused guy we all knew had turned into a red-eyed mess in eight months. By the end of the year he had been kicked out of college and was arrested for his first DUI. Still, I stayed with him. I'm not sure if it was out of sympathy, stupidity, love, pity, fear, or comfort, but nonetheless I stayed.

Meanwhile, Ed was moving on to his second year of college, smashing his goals left and right. It still made me feel incredibly proud to be his friend. He was so charismatic and kind, and he made me feel like I was the most important friend he had. Me, who little by little was starting to wither away inside from both illness and an unhealthy relationship. I was starting to feel like I didn't deserve to be important at all.

As with almost everyone, high school was an interesting time for me. Since the age of about eleven or twelve, I had always wanted to be treated like I was older. I liked hanging out with people who were older than me, and I was able to hold a conversation with teachers just as easily as with my peers. I didn't love school, mostly because I was bored and had an extremely short attention span for things I wasn't interested in.

I recently came across a note folded up into a triangle that I wrote to my friend April and that she held onto all these years. In big, bright, bubbly writing I informed April that I was in algebra class and bored to death. I went on to tell her why I thought purple was the most divine color and full of passion and energy. No wonder algebra didn't make sense to me.

I loved being with my friends though, and when I wasn't recovering from surgery, we were attached at the hip. Whenever we had a sleepover and the clock was ticking later and later into the night, I would try to teach my friends harmony parts to songs. We would start the song over and over again until someone would beg me to just let them go to sleep already. I *loved* harmony. I still *love* harmony. We could have totally nailed the harmony to "Silent Night" if those wusses had just stayed up a little longer.

Around junior year, guidance counselors started meeting with students to go over potential career choices. What we were going to do with our lives when the end of senior year came roaring upon us suddenly became a hot topic. I had some interest in health care and had already become a Certified Nursing Assistant through our school nursing program, but college didn't interest me at all. My mom, in a panic, would say things like, "Your dad and I are ready to hand you your college education on a silver platter. You better pick something and take this seriously." But I couldn't pick. You see, there was no box to check on the forms in the guidance counselor's office that said "Free-spirited writer who happens to be a sensitive Virgo and wants to feed the hungry and give the homeless homes" (shout-out to Pete and Jerry from the South Side of Chi-town). So when everyone I knew was heading off to college, I was sweeping hair off the floor at a family friend's salon.

That summer, the owner of the salon took me to the Quad Cities to assist her at a hair show. We drove two-and-a-half hours and walked through automatic sliding doors, and there—standing in the lobby of the hotel and conference center next to the fake ferns, holding cups of lukewarm vanilla cappuccinos and pulling rolling suitcases filled with mannequin heads and hairspray—were my people. I had found my box to check. *Artist*.

Later that summer I went to cosmetology school full time. Steve had moved back in with his parents and was taking some courses at a junior college nearby. He partied pretty hard, but we stayed the course together. He still showed very little interest in me and was now crabby, sometimes even mean. I was watching him change from a rough-and-tumble football player with aspirations to a not very nice man. It scared me but…are you ready for this? I felt bad for him. I know you can hear me. I will shout it louder for those of you in the back with your ears plugged and whistling away because you don't want to identify with this, but I stayed because I felt bad for him.

Steve had a bit of a rough childhood, and I blamed his behavior on that for a long time, but eventually it came to the point where I could see that he wasn't growing out of it, and now he was just plain not nice. I wasn't very secure to begin with. Even though I had started modeling in Chicago during my sophomore year, I still felt awkward and uneasy. You know that stage when you are all knees and acne? Yep. Me. One thousand percent me. Oddly enough, Steve didn't give me the confidence that I needed, he made my insecurities worse, and the worse I felt, the longer I stayed.

Throughout my high school years my mom and I also

had an interesting relationship. I'd like to blame it on the experimental hormone injections being shot into my system once every few weeks, but looking back, I now know that she *knew* I was in a very unhealthy place with my relationship, and I just would not admit it. Of course I was defensive any time there was in inkling that she was right about something. Some days I was flat out awful. My door was removed from the hinges more times than I can count, holes that my dad would patch hidden behind my Michael Jordan posters, and a fire burning so deep down inside me that I thought I could possibly explode. I was fighting to be an adult and truly thought I had all the answers. Any time my mom thought otherwise, a war broke out.

Looking back, I was holding in a lot of pain, both physical and emotional. Daughters and moms, if you're reading this and you can relate, give me a great big giant hallelujah. Now that I have a daughter of my own, I get it. I see. I understand. Our mothers are not just nagging us or out to make our lives a living hell. Nope. Nada. That's not the truth. I don't care what you say (I sound like a mom, don't I?) they are doing the best they can. They are learning too. It hit me the other day that my mom was my age now when I was a teenager. Whoa. Take that in for a second. If you are the mother of a teenager, your mom was around your age when she was raising you. Doing the best you can? Balancing work, bills, home, kids, relationships, friendships, with the slight possibility of a hot bath and a merlot before midnight? So were they. That's heavy.

Shortly after I graduated from cosmetology school, my parents took me to Fajardo, Puerto Rico on a work trip for my dad's company. The resort was set high on a cliff in the northeastern corner of the island and overlooked the point where the Atlantic Ocean and the Caribbean Sea bled into each other. From one angle of the cliff, there was the emerald-green ocean water of the Atlantic with choppy, white-capped waves as far as the eye could see. From another angle was the turquoise-blue, crystal-clear Caribbean water that was so clean you could see straight to the bottom of the sea, where the marine life lazily rocked back and forth with each gentle wave.

I was nineteen, and the drinking and gambling age there was eighteen, so I had my first "legal" sip of rum and won $500 in quarters at the resort casino. I laid in the sun from the time it came up until the time it dipped back down into the hot-pink ocean, then danced to Gloria Estefan and Bob Marley until 3 a.m. at the resort's dance club. We ate sweet crab legs and hiked rain forests and fell sound asleep at night to the lullaby of coqui frogs and soft ocean waves crashing against the smooth rocks.

While vacationing I learned of a program that sent young adults to work for a year at Puerto Rico's many resorts. It was a breath of fresh air, and I instantly knew that this was what I would do. As soon as I returned home, I was going to lay out all of my plans to return as soon as possible and soak up all of the beauty and history that Puerto Rico had to offer.

The first order of business would be breaking up with Steve. It was time, and I was ready to explore the world. You know when you look back at times in your life and map out certain exact places, times, things, songs, smells, or tastes that were *the* moment a pivotal change for you? This was a pivotal moment. I had never felt more free, more ready. I was a young adult with the support of my parents, and I was excited to start a new life. It was the first time I had felt important since Ed moved away, and I walked taller than I ever had before while stepping onto the plane to head home.

I woke up with a familiar nagging pull in my lower left side. Damn it. Another cyst. I waited for the doctor's office to open and called to get an appointment. This office was my extended family. The front desk staff was like a bunch of aunts who wore White Diamonds perfume and whispered to each other about patients coming in late; the old-school nurses were like a group of cousins to whom you could tell your life story and know it wouldn't go any further, even if they did sometimes give you a disapproving look; and the doctor was like a wise grandfather who didn't take any shit but could and would save your life in a heartbeat.

Even though I was a young woman, I loved the old-fashioned way my doctor practiced medicine. It wasn't the same as it is now, and he personally took my phone call that morning. We decided to skip straight to an ultrasound to rule out an ovarian cyst. Our game plan was as follows: if there was a cyst larger than a certain amount of centimeters, we would prep for an emergency laparoscopic procedure and remove it. If it was a small cyst, we would take a wait-and-see approach. I let my mom know that I was heading in for an ultrasound and that I would let her know what I found out. Even though I was nineteen, I was very independent and couldn't tolerate any sort of babying. Plus, this was old news. I had so many ultrasounds in the past that I could actually read the screen and knew before anyone told me whether or not I had an ovarian cyst.

So off I went on my own to the hospital. Once there and checked in, I laid in the dark room patiently as the radiology tech covered my tiny flat stomach in warm jelly and began gliding the wand over my skin just below my pierced belly button. I can recite the following conversation in my sleep.

"There is your left ovary…"

Silence.

"And there is your right ovary…"

Another long pause.

"And there, right there in the middle. Do you see that little bubble? That is your baby."

Awkward cheerfulness quickly turned into her shocked realization that I wasn't there for a prenatal visit. That was followed by a fearful look because she knew she was in trouble—she couldn't give patients that initial news.

The room spun, and voices I heard around me sounded fuzzy.

My baby. Oh shit. Bye bye, Puerto Rico. That was the end of my world.

But actually, it was just the beginning.

Chapter Three
Twenty One Down

You know that part of a thriller movie when you're watching the main character run *up* the stairs while being attacked instead of running out the front door? You scream at the TV and tell the actor that he or she is going the wrong way, but no matter how much you yell, they can't hear you. This was my conscience and me. It sounded like this: "Jonelle, you're going the wrong way. What are you doing?! Are you crazy? You are totally screwed now. Now what? Where can you go from here? Way to go, dummy."

Yep, that was me. And it was not just once when I became the character in this movie. Oh no, not just once but at least four times. Leading role: me. Talent: running right into the fire.

Steve had moved back to Carbondale to start again at SIU, and he had no phone. This was back in the day, y'all. Pay phone or bust. So I had to find a friend who had a phone, who could then tell Steve to find a phone to call me. He was twenty-two and in the middle of a Mortal Kombat marathon. He called me from a pay phone on campus, in the rain. And that is how he found out that he was going to be a dad. Did I mention that he was twenty-two?

At this point in the book I want to pivot for one second and mention that although Steve and I had a rocky start and were about to have an even rockier finish, we were both very young. That's not an excuse to allow yourself to be treated poorly, just because you're young. I also want to point that this wasn't just one person's fault. It wasn't that I was a perfect nineteen-year-old and he was a slightly older evil villain. This was two young kids dealing with some very adult issues. Two kids who did the best they knew how at that time in their lives.

Don't be too hard on yourself for your past, but don't become a victim either. This is touchy because I am not condoning bad behavior. The whole point of this book is to raise you up and help you live as your true authentic self, so I'm not telling you to allow someone to treat you in such a way that you then feel badly about yourself. What I *am* saying is that I don't hate Steve. It took me some time to get there, but I don't hate him. He was twenty-two. Let that sink in for just a second.

I packed a few things, including a tea mug in my kelly-green Seneca Irish duffle bag from high school. Why the tea mug? A few days after the baby bomb was dropped on me, I ended up doubled over in pain and spotting. My doctor knew what to do right away and started me on progesterone suppositories that were made in a small-town compound pharmacy. These supported the pregnancy and avoided a miscarriage, but they made me incredibly sick. All-day sickness, like just-the-thought-of-bacon-could-make-me-vomit kind of sick. Tea was about my only saving grace. So into the duffle bag went the tea mug.

I made the decision to move to Carbondale. Steve was living in a house on Stoker Street with a bunch of dudes who I knew from high school, and there was enough room for me but no bed. So I found someone who was getting rid of a double bed-sized air mattress, and when I arrived after a five-hour drive down south, the guys hauled it up to the tippy top of the house—the attic, where the ceiling sloped down to make a perfect-sized cubbyhole that fit the air mattress so perfectly, it was like it was built just for that reason. There was also a tiny bathroom in the attic with a shower and a little mini sink.

Hot air rises, so it was quite warm up there, but with the use of a few box fans and an open-air vent in the roof, it stayed cool enough at night to be tolerable. As long as I didn't spend any time up there during the day, I was okay.

I was still sick every day, so not having a place to cool off and rest proved to be a little challenging, but overall I was comfortable, and it would be fine until we could find our own place.

Living on Stoker Street with a bunch of guys was comparable to moving to the desert after growing up by the ocean, or maybe like moving somewhere with no electricity. Needless to say, it was an adjustment. The fridge had an array of half-empty pizza boxes and cheap beer. Once in a while if one of the parents sent a care package, there would be canned fruit and Hamburger Helper, or the devil's food…SpaghettiOs.

There was a dishwashing system too. The cheap dishes from the Dollar General would pile up, and instead of washing them in a sink of hot, soapy water, the guys would take them out back and throw them up in the air like clay pigeons and shoot them with BB guns, making my heart race and all of the neighborhood dogs go nuts. One thing I learned over the few weeks that we lived on Stoker Street was that college boys know how to get creative.

One morning I was up early to try to beat the warm spring sun. I had an interview at the JCPenney salon later that day and needed to hand wash my clothes and let them hang dry. As I dragged my tired body down the stairs, I heard a few loud pops and glass breaking. I hit the floor. A drive-by? An attacker? Maybe a drunk college kid in the wrong house?

As the popping quieted, I slowly pushed myself back up off the floor but kept my eyes shut so tight I could see spots. I finally opened them and walked slowly and carefully around the corner to find one of the guys on the back steps doing the morning dishes—Stoker Street style. As my eyes refocused, I caught a glimpse of something shiny and white flying up into the air before exploding into powdery shards of glass. My tea mug.

This was the first time I remember crying in Carbondale. The tears didn't stop for two years, and when I finally emerged on the other side of them, I would find myself staring in the mirror at the image of a now grown woman with empty eyes and shallow breathing that was just enough to keep her going from day to day.

We didn't have any money. Like, none at all. Steve was still in college and working a little part-time job at a telemarketing company on the outskirts of town. We had one car, mine, but my parents paid the car insurance on it. I needed a job desperately.

The first interview at the JCPenney salon was more of a computer questionnaire that asked things like "How would you handle a customer if they became angry while making a return?" I must have given the right answers because I passed and was thrilled to be asked to return a few days later to meet the salon manager.

I threw on my freshly hand-washed black pants, which were just starting to feel a little snug around the waist. I had hung them to dry over the shower curtain, but now they had a crease in the center of the legs where the curtain imprinted its mark. Note to self: buy an iron.

I had enough time for a bowl of cereal, then out the door I went. I was to meet the manager in the salon just inside the back entrance to JCP. The salon was brightly lit with long fluorescent lights that reflected off of the shiny black floor tiles. Rows of glass retail shelves housed perfect rows of Matrix hair products, and the entire salon smelled like coconuts.

Imagine, if you will, the moment in movie fantasies when a beautiful, tall woman with flowing blonde hair moves in slow motion through a room with a smile straight out of a Colgate commercial. That is exactly what happened when Kelly Brown walked around the corner to greet me. I was starstruck. She was like a real-life Barbie but even more perfect. She looked like Brooke Shields, but prettier and softer and calmer. I actually don't know how soft and calm Brooke Shields is, but I'm pretty sure Kelly could outdo her.

Kelly had a slight Southern drawl that made words like

"soda" and "highlight" sound as sweet as honey. I was instantly embarrassed by my pants and wanted to explain to her that I was actually raised really well, and if I had lived at home my pants would have been pressed and smelled like Snuggle, but Stoker Street didn't have any fabric softener... or a washing machine for that matter, and please, please, please don't judge me by my pants because I am so much more than them... But in true Kelly fashion, she didn't even look at my pants, and she immediately made me feel at ease.

Kelly asked me to highlight her hair as a "hands-on interview" because she needed a touch-up anyway. She was easy to talk to and I was finally starting to relax a little. About ten minutes into the highlight interview, I could feel the cereal from earlier churning in my stomach. *Oh my God. I can't throw up now. She'll know that I'm pregnant and she won't hire me!* But as luck would have it, pregnancy sickness doesn't care what time it is or where you are or that you are in the middle of highlighting your potential new boss's hair. Nope. It doesn't care. So I excused myself and practically ran out of the salon. A few minutes later as I was splashing my face with cold water and rinsing my mouth out, sweet Kelly pushed open the door and stood there looking at me with concern on her face.

"Are you okay? Are you ill?" she asked.

It was all I could do to mutter out a squeaky, "No," with tears starting to well up in my eyes.

"Are you pregnant?" she whispered.

No words came out of my mouth, only a big teary nod.

A smile slowly spread across her face and her gentle eyes lit up.

"Oh my goodness, that is wonderful!" she almost shouted as she clasped her hands in front of her in excitement. "Well, you're going to need a job to raise this baby, so come on, let's get your paperwork going. Welcome to the team!" she said matter-of-factly but also with a little squeal at the end. This was the first moment when I realized that I wanted to be just like Kelly someday.

The back of the salon shared a wall with the food court in the center of the mall. My shift started at 8 a.m., and every morning I could smell the cookies being baked at the Mrs. Fields cookie stand on the other side of the wall. On the days that I made tips, I would walk to the food court on my lunch break and order a baked potato with broccoli from Great Steak and a peanut butter cookie sandwich with thick dark-chocolate frosting squished in the middle. I would take my lunch back to the break room and slowly eat the cookie first, then the broccoli, and finally the potato.

One afternoon a manager from another department came in to warm up his lunch. He greeted me with bright eyes and a cheerful hello. He introduced himself as Austin, and I found myself in an instant conversation about where I came from and how I liked my first few days. Austin told me that his wife, Kathy, was also pregnant and due a few months before me. Kathy was a psychology professor at the university, and I made a mental note to not mention the accommodations at Stoker Street because I could tell right away, even though we'd just met, that Austin would worry.

I was right. Austin worried about everything, and he and Kathy would end up becoming dear friends of mine who took me under their wing but never made me feel less than capable. Years later, Austin and Kathy would make the trip up north to be with me when I married my first husband. We lost touch a little after that, and I like to think of them as angels who walked with me until they knew I was strong enough to walk by myself. Once in a while we connect, and it's always incredible to hear about their daughter and their lives and catch them up on all that I've got going on as well. These are the kind of people whose existence in your world you should never question. They are proof that the universe will send you the right people at the right time.

Everyone in your life is there for a reason—some to teach you a lesson, some to support you, some to love you, some to challenge you and help you move up to the next level or to a higher vibration. Trust that everyone put in your path is there for a very important reason. Sometimes it's sad to see them go when their job with you is done, but try to look back with a full heart as you start to realize that they left you with a gift.

My pregnancy was fairly uneventful. A month after I started the job at JCP, Steve and I found an apartment across town and moved in. Rent was cheap and the apartment building was directly across from the high school, so it felt safe as well. There were two apartments upstairs and two apartments downstairs. Ours was a downstairs unit with two bedrooms, a tiny kitchen with pea-green linoleum, and a bay window with rust-colored metal blinds. Below the bay window was a wall air conditioner that cooled the living room and kitchen but left the bedrooms in the back hot and sticky in the southern Illinois heat.

Since we had no furniture, my family was gracious enough to get us started. My aunt gave us a pull-out couch and a little kitchen table that folded down on each side to fit into our tiny kitchen. My parents gave us a blue reclining chair that had lived in their living room for years and was ready for a new home. We also got a particle board entertainment center from Walmart, my bedroom set from my bedroom back home, a TV from someone, and my stereo system that I got for Christmas my junior year. If I had any extra tip money I would go to Walmart and buy a new couch cover and shower curtain to spruce things up a little. At night you could hear cockroaches scurrying across the linoleum floor with their little legs that sounded like fingernails being drummed across a hard surface.

I was really starting to show by this time and was uncomfortable in any position, not to mention being hot *all* of the damn time. Pregnancy was not becoming on me in any sense of the word. My nose spread across my face and made my eyes look squinty, and I could barely walk across the room without one of my knees giving out. Imagine a newborn calf trying to walk. Now imagine said calf has a really huge nose, a serious case of hormonal acne, and is nauseous all the livelong day. Cute, eh? So because of how hot the bedrooms got, I would pull out the bed in the couch every night and crank up the wall air conditioner. That little unit could cool off the room, but it smelled like must and mold and made my already uncomfortably large nose completely close shut with congestion. It was a tradeoff though because Steve usually snored away in the hot bedroom and didn't like it when I made him any warmer than he already was. So I slept by myself and I was A-okay with that.

My due date was November sixth and it was now mid-September. I turned twenty on September third, and although my birthday was usually marked by falling leaves and cooler temperatures, southern Illinois was still blazing hot. Most of my friends were heading back to college to start their sophomore year. I could see the buzz around me since I was residing in a college town. Living in a college town when you are not in college but the same age as everyone living there because they're going to college is a bizarre feeling. Add a watermelon-sized stomach to the mix and you get some strange looks.

Work was going well. My coworkers threw me a surprise baby shower, and my friends and family back home threw me one too, so now our second bedroom was filled with a brand new white crib, a changing table, and a dresser that was filled with perfectly folded tiny baby clothes. We still didn't have a washer and dryer, so a couple times a week I lugged the tall green laundry basket to the car and drive to the laundromat, wash and dry a few loads, fill the basket back up, and lug everything home. When my belly grew too big to carry the basket, I dragged it. Just as the basket was getting too heavy to drag, I found the holiest of holy laundry lands: the drive-up, drop-off laundry window. It was a little more expensive than doing it myself, but this was a luxury I was willing to spend a few extra dollars on. Steve was going to class all day and working at the telemarketing job at night. We still shared my car, so I would pick him up at 10 p.m. when his shift was over.

Halloween in Carbondale was known for outrageous parties, but the only party I was having on Halloween 1998 was the one celebrating the end of my pregnancy nearing. My doctor saw me the morning of the thirty-first for my final prenatal appointment. Dr. H was a *slow*-moving, large, round man with glasses. He didn't get excited about much, but this particular day he walked into the exam room wearing a giant ladybug costume complete with black tights and a headband with round antennas poking out of the top. After checking my cervix, he informed me that it would be any day now. I remember saying a quick prayer asking God to make the baby come the next day so that the first thing it would see wouldn't be a giant male ladybug.

A few short days later I woke up early in the morning with sore inner thighs, like I had used a Thighmaster or ridden a horse the night before. By that afternoon I was starting to feel the rhythmic tightening of contractions but nothing that seemed to be in a pattern of any sort. By early evening we decided it was time to head to the hospital, where they put me in a room to observe the monitors they had hooked me up to. Around 10 p.m. a nurse came in and told me that I was dilated to four but not contracting regularly. She suggested that I go home and take a warm bath or go walk around "Walsmart" for a while. No, really, that's how she said it. So being twenty and having no idea what to expect (even though I read *What to Expect When You're Expecting* from front to back) and even though Heidi Murkoff didn't say anything about leaving the hospital, I put my clothes back on and headed home.

Once home, Steve threw some mustard chicken on the mini grill on the sidewalk out front and I sank down into a warm bath. Steve thought it would be a good idea if I had some protein, and even though I hated mustard, I planned on having a few bites when I got out of the bath… but I couldn't get out of the bathtub. I relaxed enough that I went into active labor before the chicken was even warm. The rhythmic contracting quickly turned into sheer tearing pain shooting down each leg, across my abdomen, and into my back. Soaking wet and slippery, Steve tried his best to lift me out of the bathtub with no luck. Finally, in between contractions, I was able to hoist myself out and put a t-shirt over my head.

Steve got me to the car and threw a blanket over my lap. Each contraction was coming faster and harder, and with every tightening of my uterus my head flew back like there was a pulley attached to each body part. I didn't recognize the sounds coming out of my own mouth but knew they were helping ease the pain.

We only lived a few blocks from the Carbondale Memorial Hospital, and Steve ran over the curb as we pulled up to the emergency room entrance. A patient care tech met us at the car door with a wheelchair and ran me to the elevator to send me up to the OB floor. Everything from there is a blur. My blood pressure was a little high, but that was normal with pain. Nine centimeters, more sheer pain—and too late for an epidural.

Grunting, pleading, crying, begging for help, I was wheeled into a delivery room, helped into a gown and onto the delivery table. An IV was started in my left arm, and finally the warm, woozy feeling of pain medication hitting my bloodstream took over. It was now 3 a.m. and Dr. H lazily wandered in. Dilated to ten, it was time to push. Baby was sunny side up, and its hard head sat directly on my sciatic nerve, causing back pain that can only be described as hot, burning cattle prods being jabbed at me over and over.

An hour and twenty minutes of pushing later and my son was born. They probably handed him to me, but I have no recollection because the Fentanyl they pushed into my IV was causing some sort of adverse reaction. I wondered what they were doing right now in Puerto Rico. Probably not this.

"He stopped breathing." These were the next words I remember hearing. The sun had come up, and my mom and Memere had arrived after driving through the night just a few minutes after Daniel was born. I was starting to come to my senses a little, and a nice nursing assistant had brought me a tray with eggs and bacon. It was the first time in nine months that I was able to eat breakfast without throwing up. It was heavenly.

All at once the door to the hospital room flew open, and Steve slid in on one foot like a baseball player barely making it to first base. A nurse was hot on his heels and slid in next. "He stopped breathing and he turned blue in the nursery, and I was pounding on the window and they finally saw him," he said, breathing hard.

The nurse all but pushed Steve aside and, breathless herself, told me that he was, in fact, breathing and just fine but that the pediatrician was going to run some tests to see why he had turned a little dusky. I don't know if it was the Fentanyl or the bacon, but I slowly nodded and continued to chew. All at once the room felt unfamiliar and I didn't quite feel like I was in my body. This is the earliest memory I have of experiencing what I know now is anxiety. Thankfully, the pediatrician was able to clear us to go home a couple of days later, and off we went as a family of three.

The next few days were a blur as they are with any new baby. Up all night, learning to nurse, nipple cream, newborn diapers, more nipple cream, rinse and repeat. I was so busy that I hadn't noticed that I really wasn't having much postpartum bleeding. After all, I had never been through this before, and the chapter in the pregnancy book on postpartum was short and sweet. I had also moved on to Dr. Sears' baby bible and was reading up on pumping and freezing. Just like any new mom, my focus had shifted from taking care of myself to taking care of a new tiny screaming human.

This is the part of the book where I introduce you to three words you'll read throughout the rest of these chapters: trusting your gut. I know most of us get that feeling deep down in our bellies, that ache of knowing, but I also know that because of our conscious self, we push that ache down. We tell ourselves that we are worriers, paranoid, crazy. Sound familiar?

Trusting your gut instinct is one of the most crucial of survival traits. The brain uses a combination of logic and emotion when making a decision. Not only does it not serve you in any way to ignore these instincts, but it can be downright dangerous, as you're about to find out.

By day five of the postpartum period, and we were in the swing of things. I no longer cried when Daniel peed on me while I changed his diaper. He no longer cried when he was done drinking his bottle after I discovered how to push all of the extra air out of the bag holding his dinner. We had this thing down pat.

My mom had stayed for a couple of days to help me and had left to go home. The same day she left, Steve's mom had come to visit and was now getting ready to leave after dinner. Steve, his mom, and I had dinner at around 5 p.m. and I didn't eat much because I just wasn't feeling very well. It had been a whirlwind of guests and family the last five days, so I figured I was just tired.

I went to lie down for a bit and woke up around 7 p.m. to a warm oozing feeling running down my leg. I thought maybe the baby had peed on me again, but once I woke up a little more, I discovered that I had some blood dripping down my leg. Steve's mom had left an hour or so prior, so it was just Steve, Daniel, and me. I walked to the bathroom and cleaned myself up a little. Huh. Maybe just a little end of the postpartum bleeding, since I hadn't had much all week.

I went into the living room and sat on our blue recliner to flip through some pages of the *What to Expect* book. Maybe somewhere it talked about being five days postpartum and what to expect.

Whoosh. Another gush. This one was a little bigger. I stood up and found that the blood had soaked through my pants and onto the fabric of the chair. I panicked and threw a hand towel over the circular stain and rushed off to the bathroom. This time there was a blood clot around the size of a quarter. It was 8 p.m. on Sunday, and the doctor's office wasn't open. I would have to wait and see how things went.

I flipped through the pages of the pregnancy book, this time in the bathroom, to see what I should do about this. *Gush*. Another blood clot, this time the size of a small plum. I yelled for Steve and asked him if he thought this was normal after having five days with hardly any bleeding.

By 9 p.m. we both decided, with our young and inexperienced minds, that it did make sense. That maybe there was a lot of blood just kind of sitting up there, and now it was finally making its way out. Still, I called my mom and she asked if she should turn around and come back. She had been home for only an hour or so, but she must have heard the panic in my voice because she told me that she was going to get a few things together and head back down.

By 11 p.m. I was passing clots the size of grapefruits, and every time I stood up, gushes of blood came flowing out like a river. I told Steve that I thought we should check in to the ER and see if something was wrong. I was feeling a little woozy, mostly because of the anxiety that hit every time more blood clots surfaced.

Steve packed up the baby and me, and we headed back to the same ER doors that I went through five days prior. A nurse took me straight to the back and put me in a gown. There was blood on the floor in a little pattern of dots, like in a horror movie when someone is stabbed and doesn't know it yet.

The nurse put me on a bed with stirrups, and I sat on absorbent bed pads to soak up the blood. She looked concerned and told me a few times that the doctor would be right in. Finally, after what felt like an eternity, the doctor knocked twice and entered the room. I could tell right away that he was cocky. Remember that instinct thing? It's a great truth teller. First impressions are everything, and he made a horrible one. He had the personality of a wet washcloth, but as long as he took care of me, none of that mattered. He did a quick examination and pressed on my belly a few times, flipped the exam light off, and explained that he believed I was having normal postpartum bleeding and that I should call my OBGYN in the morning if I was still having a problem. He would get the nurse to get my paperwork together, and I could go home.

I would like to explain here that my trust in medical professionals has always been high, and so has my respect for their knowledge. So I didn't think to question him about sending me home. My gut was shooting off fireworks and telling me that something was very wrong, but I reminded myself that I was just a twenty-year-old girl with no college education who happened to be on state insurance and that my opinion didn't matter. Oh sweet girl. If only you knew how big your voice would grow. How much your opinion *did* matter.

I tried to put some pants back on to head home. The second I stood up, *GUSH*, another large blood clot splattered all over the emergency room floor. The nurse holding my discharge papers told us that she would be right back, that maybe the doctor should take another look. She returned a few minutes later with her head hung low, like she knew what she was about to do was wrong but was only following protocol, and handed me discharge papers.

"He said to give you these," she said sheepishly and handed me a stack of stark white towels.

So I left holding towels between my legs to soak up the blood that was still pouring out of me. My gut screamed, "Go back, don't leave! He's wrong!" But my mind told my gut to just be quiet in case they heard me.

By the time we got home from the ER, it was 2 a.m. and my mom was only a couple of hours out from arriving. I sat in the already wrecked chair with my legs up and my back reclined, holding towels between my legs. If I held perfectly still and didn't move, I could sleep for a minute or two at a time. My head was starting to feel a little fuzzy, and every time I stood up, blood clots that were now the size of mini Nerf footballs would fall into my pants.

It was 5 a.m. I was the color of the pasty white apartment paint on the living room wall. My mom arrived looking ragged, worried, and tired. She took one look at me and told me we needed to go back to the ER. My gut stepped in to say, "She's right, Jonelle, we need to go back," but I reminded my mom that they sent me home and told me to call my OBGYN in the morning. They would open at eight, so we only had a few hours left until I could call.

At 8 a.m. on the dot I called the office. I explained to the nurse all that had occurred, and she informed me that my doctor was on vacation but another doctor could see me at one. I told her that I would be dead by then. Silence, and then an annoyed voice that said, "Then you need to go back to the ER." Okay, that was three people: my mom, the nurse, and my gut. So my mom stayed with Daniel while Steve hauled me back to the ER doors for the third time in a week.

A new shift had started, and bright sunshine and the smell of black coffee filled the area. Steve was practically carrying me in because I had zero strength left. The triage nurse took one look at me and called for help. Everything after that point is a blur.

I was poked and examined, and nurses tried to start IVs. There were ten people or more in the room, and everyone was rushing around. I was too weak to lift my head. Someone yelled for me to keep my eyes open, but it was just too hard to do. Pages were going off over the loudspeaker, and I realized they were for me. Still, I couldn't open my eyes. I felt fuzzy and warm, and I was actually okay with sleeping because I was so tired, but someone kept yelling at me to wake up. A nurse knelt in front of me, inches away from my face, and in a tone that I have yet to hear again, she practically cried, "Open your eyes!" So I did because sheesh, she was really upset.

I opened my eyes and took one look at her and everything came rushing back—the pain in my head that was now pounding, the warm gushing feeling of blood, the nausea that was making my head spin round and round.

"Am I going to die?" I squeaked out as the anxiety came flooding back with every tick of the clock.

"We are going to do everything we can for you," she replied.

Whoa. She didn't say no. She didn't tell me that I was going to be just fine. She didn't know if I was going to be okay and she wasn't going to lie to me. I had a six-day-old baby. I was still nursing him. How was my mom feeding him? Why was everyone still rushing? *Oh my God, I am going to die.*

I laid my head back again, and this time a petite female physician calmly said, "Jonelle, open your eyes, dear. We need to talk options and I need your consent for surgery. We are preparing an OR right now, and I'm waiting for the OBGYN on call to give me the okay to send you down. In the meantime, we are going to start you on some Pitocin. We believe you either have a tear in your uterus or some tissue left that is causing your bleeding. The medicine will help to clamp down your uterus and stop the bleeding. If this doesn't work right away, we're going to have to perform a hysterectomy. Can we have your consent to do all of those things?"

"Yes. Yes, you can."

The Pitocin was started along with some kind of iron, and just like that, as quickly as it began, the bleeding stopped.

The staff allowed my mom to bring my baby to me so that I could feed him. She had been giving him sugar water that the nursery sent home, and he had been screaming and hungry for a while now. The hospital gave me the choice of going home or staying the night for observation, but if I stayed I couldn't keep the baby with me, so I decided to go home.

Round one of getting me up and out of bed was tricky. The nurse put me in a wheelchair and wheeled me out to the car, but as soon as I stood up, I fainted. Back into the ER, where I stayed for another six hours and recovered until I could go home and continue my recovery.

The apartment that had once looked like a murder scene was now clean and relaxing. My mom stayed for a few days and made me steak and spinach to bring my iron back up. I took handfuls of prescription iron and other medications to keep my uterus contracted. This was in November, and it took me until Easter to feel good enough to do anything. I couldn't go back to work, so it was just pale me and a colicky baby hanging out while Steve continued to complete his education.

I wish I could shout this from the rooftops with a megaphone: trust your gut. If something doesn't feel right, get a second opinion, run the other way. Don't go home and let yourself practically bleed to death because you are convinced that someone is more educated than you, so that must mean they are smarter. Educated and smart are two different things, darlin'. In every aspect of life there will come a time when you have to advocate for yourself. Let your voice be heard. Doesn't feel like anyone can hear you? Get louder. I have learned along the way in so many situations how to use my voice for more than singing. Yes, sometimes it takes bravery, fearlessness, and courage to stand up and say that something isn't right, but you have to listen to that inner voice asking you to protect yourself.

As Daniel grew, I thought it would be nice if we could find a bigger space to live in. There was a house around the corner that was in a quiet neighborhood tucked into the back part of Carbondale. Old pine bushes surrounded the house, and a little concrete patio made for a nice outdoor space. There was a large kitchen, a one-car garage, a large laundry room, three bedrooms, one bathroom, and a nice-sized living room. It was $500 a month, a little more than the $425 we were paying for the apartment, but it seemed well worth it, considering the space we would have.

Steve was at school most of the time and studying with his old dorm roommate the rest of the time. We didn't spend much time together, and by the time Daniel was five months old or so, we had grown apart. He seemed annoyed with having a family and was gone most of the time anyway. My gut (there's that word again) was telling me that it was time to move forward and take some steps to getting back my own life, so I applied for a job at a little boutique salon near the hippie part of town. I called it the hippie part of town because it was a little neighborhood with cobblestone roads and a tiny little grocery store/deli called the Neighborhood Co-op. The co-op had old wooden floors and smelled like herbs and patchouli. They served things like hummus and chai tea before hummus and chai tea were cool.

I felt like a superstar when I was offered the job at Hair Brains, the coolest little salon ever. The manager was from a town near my hometown, and she made me feel like I was home. Some of the girls would sit in the back room and sing harmony to songs by Reba or to "Amazing Grace" and would ask me to join in. I had forgotten over the year of hauling laundry to the laundromat and trying not to die from postpartum hemorrhaging how much I loved to sing. I hadn't sung harmony since my sleepover days, and it was like my soul was bursting out of my chest with every note. Carol, our manager, would get teary-eyed and ask me and a couple of the other girls to "sing it again." It made me feel amazing to be able to touch someone's heart just by singing a harmony part.

The more time I spent at the salon, the more I felt like myself again, but I was only able to work one day a week due to Steve's class schedule. But things at home were already at their worst anyway. I was finding my voice in more ways than just singing, and I started to stand up for myself, which Steve didn't know what to do with, so he would just tell me to "shut the hell up" because what the hell did I know anyway. He was "the one in college after all."

I'm not saying that I was a good fighter, because I wasn't. I had slammed so many doors in my time that I should have been in slammer's jail or something. But when things started happening, like soda being poured on my head or phones being ripped out of the wall when I would threaten to call the police after a few particularly bad fights, I knew we were going down a very bad road.

One evening I had picked up some ground beef from Walmart. Cooking was one of my favorite things to do, and I would sit with note cards and write out recipes while Daniel napped. I was going to make sloppy joes. I had the ketchup bottle out and was browning the beef. Daniel, in his high chair eating rice puffs, kept throwing his snacks on the ground. I had to stop what I was doing to pick them up, and it became a game. The next thing I knew, the beef had browned but looked like long, thin worms from the way it was pressed into the package, and now it was too late to break it up.

Around that time, Steve came in and looked into the pan with an expression of disgust. "I'm not eating that, it's disgusting," he said with snark.

I snapped back and told him to stop being such a diva, then continued cooking. All of a sudden I felt something gooey and warm dripping down my hair and into my ears and eyes. Ketchup. He had dumped ketchup on me. Daniel was screaming because I'm sure my appearance scared him. I know it wasn't my reaction that scared him because I couldn't move. I just stood there speechless, dripping with Heinz and silently praying for a way out. Steve slammed the door and left.

This was the beginning of many nights of knock-down, drag-out fights. We had holes in our walls, holes in our pride, broken spirits, and broken glass everywhere. One night when Daniel had a high fever and I needed our car to take him to the hospital, I found Steve in his old roommate's apartment with a girl on his lap. I slapped Steve in the ear so hard that even after all these years, I still wonder whether or not his hearing was affected.

Whenever I would have a bad moment or when Daniel could feel my tension and it was just the two of us, I would put on a Dixie Chicks CD and rock Daniel on my hip. We would go back and forth through the living room, singing every word to every song, and then starting it over and doing it all again. Daniel would hang off of my hip chewing on the nipple of a colorful apple juice-filled bottle, completely content being part of my concert. "Let Him Fly" was my favorite song. I would sing it at the top of my lungs. At that point in my life, Daniel and the Hair Brains girls were the only people I had to sing in front of.

During this time my only saving grace was Hair Brains and Ed. Remember him? Ed and I had been in touch a few months after Daniel was born, when I called him to tell him that I had a baby boy. We talked on the phone quite a bit, and he would tell me where he was going next with his sports career. He was the hardest worker I knew, and I wanted him to be proud of me too, even though I was living a secret life of hell.

Ed knew though. He asked me several times if I wanted him to come and get me. Yes, I did. Desperately, actually. But I was too afraid of change. After all, I had now been with Steve for six years and he was all I knew. I would tell Ed about the fights that Steve and I had, and I could practically hear him shake his head through the phone, but his hands were tied because he respected my wishes. He still made me feel as important as he did the day I met him, and he had no idea how much that helped me hang on to a thread of my dignity. Once in a while Ed would offer to let me come to his house and stay. A few times I made plans to go, but I always chickened out, a decision that would haunt me for years to come.

The staff at work started to notice too. Sometimes I used my tip money to buy a joint from a coworker because I felt like if I could keep Steve "chill", we might not fight. My manager gently prodded me a few times, asking if I was okay, but I had become so good at the masquerade that sometimes I even tricked myself into believing that everything was fine.

One evening while I was at work, I got a walk in. This wasn't just any walk in, this was a life-changing, about-to-become-lifelong-friends walk in. If you ever question destiny, read this part over and over again.

Her name was Megha, and she stood there with mounds of jet-black hair halfway down her back. Her dark skin glistened and her smile was blinding. There was something angelic about her. Calm. Peaceful. I was instantly drawn in, not unlike my meeting with Kelly Brown. There was an instant connection of souls. She was pre-planned by something bigger than us, intended to be there at this exact moment.

She held a baby on her hip, only a year older than mine, with ebony hair that matched her own. I can't even remember the conversation we had that day, but I know we made plans for a playdate for the babies and to share our recipes with each other. She would share her Indian recipes, and I would share my French ones.

It was around this time that I learned about praying specifically and setting intentions. Only I didn't realize then that that's what I was doing. So what is praying specifically? It is simply praying for something very clearly. It helps us to define our needs. So every single night I would ask God to put me on the path I was meant to be on. Every night for months and months I would ask the same thing. I knew in my gut that there was more for me, I just didn't know what yet.

At this time, I also began setting my intention. Merriam-Webster defines an intention as "the thing that you plan to do or achieve: an aim or purpose." Your intentions give you greater control of your life, and that is something I needed in my life, which was quickly spinning out of control. No, I take that back. It had spun off of its axis and had fallen into a deep black hole. So I set my intention nightly too.

I imagined a large stage with a light show so bright you could see it for miles—an outdoor venue filled with concert goers walking up the lawn to sit on blankets or finding their seats down in the pit. The drummer took the stage first, and with every hit of the bass pedal, the lights changed color and became pastel in the smoke being released by the smoke machines. The crowd would go wild. Next, the guitar player stepped in front and cranked out the dirtiest, sexiest intro to our own cover of Guns N' Roses' "Paradise City" (don't ask, it just happened to be that song). Just as the drummer hit the last of the intro, right on beat, I appeared from a lift that was pushing me up through the bottom of the stage. I was just a silhouette of myself in the smoke and lights, but the crowd grew even louder, and it would be so deafening that I couldn't hear the guitar player, but I could see the energy moving through his fingers onto the strings. And then the show started.

This is setting an intention. Feeling it, seeing it, hearing it, tasting it. Knowing it inside and out. Playing it in your head like a movie or a past memory that is so vivid, you can feel the way it changes your heartbeat. I had been envisioning this scene since the days of my brother pulling back the curtains, but somewhere along the line it was lost. Now these little glimpses showed themselves and let me escape into a fantasy world of being something I would be proud of… And then the baby would cry, and I would wake up in my dark room in Carbondale, sleeping next to someone who I didn't even like.

Megha (Meg) and I became fast friends. She had invited me to her home for our first playdate/cooking date, and I was heading over with Daniel in tow. As I left the outskirts of town and turned into the subdivision, I started to panic. I was in one of the nicest neighborhoods in Carbondale. These were huge, beautiful homes made of brick and stone with multiple peaks on their roofs. Large, perfectly manicured yards hugged each grand front porch, and stamped concrete driveways led to carriage-style cedar garage doors. The kind of garages that had not one, not two, but three spaces to park in. *Oh no. I'm going to look so out of place with my Walmart shoes and Daniel's hand-me-down baby clothes.* I was out of my league.

I don't know why people who have more money than me make me feel insecure. Meg certainly never made me feel that way. It's just a deep insecurity that I'm still learning to handle.

To my surprise, Meg didn't have much furniture. She and her husband, a neurosurgeon, had just moved to Carbondale, and she was just getting settled. I can still picture her tiny little frame in this huge house with no couches. It makes me giggle when I think about how worried I was. We were all just trying to get by.

The babies played with toys, and Meg took me to her kitchen, where she lit the burner under a pot and put in a dollop of ghee, clarified butter. She showed me how to roast cream of wheat to bring out its nutty flavor. She had dissolved sugar in hot water, and she slowly poured that into the pot, stirring and stirring until a fragrant, thick, gritty cream was made. She then poured it into a pan and let it cool. I can't remember exactly what we topped it with, but I think it was golden raisins and slivered almonds and maybe yellow saffron or some cardamom. Either way it was the most delicious sooji ka halwa I have ever had.

We talked in great detail about our lives and where we had come from before our predestined meeting in this southern city. It didn't take Meg long to see that I was in a bad place. She wanted to help me, I could tell, but she wasn't sure how to help without overstepping. I was crying inside for her kind sister-like love and felt like I had met someone who could finally push me to do better.

A few months into our friendship Meg and I were going to meet up at a bakery in town for breakfast. I was under a lot of stress this particular morning because Steve and I got into a fight over something that same morning, and as I was holding Daniel on my hip, a big three-wick candle whizzed past my head. It crashed through the wall and fell to the ground. The candle was so heavy that the glass candle holder didn't even chip. I was frozen with fear and kept my mouth shut and head down. Steve had class that morning, and I knew I would be better off with him there than at home, so I still gave him a ride. As I was dropping him off at school, we got into yet another argument when I asked him how long he would be. He didn't like to be bothered with questions like that because how was he supposed to know? By this time in our relationship I had become really exhausted with these kinds of responses, and I'm sure I said something snotty, which in turn bought me a whole can of Coke dumped over my head.

I still headed to the bakery where Meg and a mutual friend who had joined our playgroup were waiting for me. Within minutes the ladies knew it was time, and they offered to help me get out while Steve was still in class. I could feel my heart pounding. I knew that it was now or never. I kept hearing the whizzing of the candle going by my head and feeling the hard chunks of hair that had dried together in a sugary matted mess. They were right—it was time.

I drove home and just kind of stood in the house, overwhelmed as to where to start. Meg had followed me home, and she started directing the show. She started coaching me, saying things like, "Here, put these in shoeboxes, grab only what you need. Bring anything valuable. You can get the rest later. Don't forget diapers and food. You'll need most of your clothes, they can go in garbage bags." We moved swiftly, and it almost felt as if we were robbers in the middle of a burglary, knocking off a house by stealing the essentials. We shoved as much as we could into the trunk of the car and took one last look around. Meg looked me in the eye, gave me a warm hug and said, "Go!" So I did. I went.

Once I hit the highway heading north, each mile felt more and more freeing. I made it about 100 miles when it dawned on me that I didn't have enough money to get home. I called my aunt, who was the VP of a transportation company, and she issued me a special type of check for truck drivers' fuel and cash advances. It was a series of numbers and codes that I would give the fuel desk, and they would give me a code for fuel and some cash. I could pay her back sometime, she said. She could hear in my voice that I needed help, and no questions were asked.

I stood in line at the truck stop fuel desk with a baby on my hip and bright red cheeks. Adrenaline pumped through my body, helping me ignore the ringing cell phone in my pocket coming from a pay phone on campus. Steve was probably wondering where the hell I was. He really had no idea that today was the last day I would allow something to be dumped on my head.

I fueled up and bought a meal at Cracker Barrel, which I shared with Daniel. Just me and a baby out on the highway, 300 miles away from our new start. When we were ready to hit the road again, Jo Dee Messina's song "Bye Bye" came on the radio. In it, she talks about tearing off her rearview mirror and never looking back. So I literally tore off my rearview mirror. That's one of my friend's favorite stories to tell. It was a long ride back north with no rearview mirror, but one thing is for sure—it kept me looking ahead instead of back.

Chapter 4
Not your Doll

ROADS ARE FUNNY. NOT FUNNY *ha ha* but funny in a weird and quirky way. You can be cruising along just fine and the next thing you know, there is a curve in the road that corkscrews around like a snake. Most of the time there's a big yellow warning sign with black squiggly lines that represents what's ahead, but sometimes we don't see the sign, and out of nowhere our once smooth and straight blacktopped road is now a jagged, dangerously curvy gravel road and you're losing control.

How did this happen? You were just on a straight road, windows down, listening to Aerosmith's "Cryin'" and now you're in a ditch, your car flipped over on its hood, bleeding from your forehead. The curves got you. You're not dead… but you're pretty dazed. What do you do? You can't sit in your upside down car. That's not safe. So you do the only thing you can do: climb out of the broken window, call for help, and start to let it all sink in.

The beginning of this chapter is the smooth road. Let's see if you can figure out when I hit the gravel.

A few weeks after moving back in with my parents, we decided it would be best if I had a place of my own to stay. I had just started a job that was offered to me by my aunt at the transportation company she managed. The same company that gave me the money to get home. I gladly accepted.

My dad knew of a couple in town who were selling their duplex and offered to buy it from them so that I could rent it from him. A generous offer, and one that as a parent of adult children, I hope I can someday offer as grand of a gesture if needed.

The duplex was a peachy-tan tri-level with a deck on the front and a deck on the back. The one-car garage was under the upstairs bedroom and led into a ground-floor laundry room. A few steps up and you were in the kitchen and living room, and a few more up and there were two bedrooms and a full bathroom. The couple who had lived here had faux painted the kitchen and living room and wallpapered one focus wall with thick vertical-striped wallpaper.

I didn't bring any furniture with me from Carbondale during my quick escape, so I had to think fast. My dad, who had worked for years as a financial advisor, had taken some of my brother's and my graduation money and invested it into some mutual funds and stocks. My stock was currently doing well, and I was able to pull out enough money to buy a burgundy overstuffed couch and chair set, a TV, a race car toddler bed for Daniel, and two Polk Audio speakers. I *loved* this duplex. It stood for so many things for me, but mainly freedom. I was working full time and had health insurance and perks from the company, like Nextel cell phones that doubled as walkie-talkies.

I was twenty-one years old and Daniel was one. Both of my parents were working, so I needed to find childcare. After one awful experience with an in-home babysitter, we found an older couple in town who had watched kids for years. Anne and Bill. Their son, Craig, a few years older than me, had gone to high school with me and was the cousin of a good friend of mine. I knew this family was good and felt blessed when they took Daniel in. Anne and Bill would end up being family to me, helping me raise my son, breaking him of his pacifier, potty training him, and feeding me dinner when I would get home too late from work to feed myself. They were like having extra grandparents, and they loved Daniel and me like their own. That was who they were and what kind of people they were. They made everyone feel like family.

It was also here at this home that I would run into my next big life lesson. Like literally. I ran right into him.

I was pulling into Anne and Bill's around 6 p.m. after work one night, and Craig and his friend Sam were sitting on the front porch. It had been a rough day at work. I had sent a truck to Columbus, Ohio instead of Columbus City, Iowa, and my boss had thrown the bad call brick at me. The bad call brick was a Nerf-type brick with the words "BAD CALL" printed in big black letters across the front. If you did something dumb you didn't get yelled at, but instead you got the bad call brick. I was tired and ready to grab Daniel and get home when Sam informed me that I had something leaking out of my car and it didn't look good.

Great! That was the icing on the cake. What was I going to do now? Sam told me he could take my car, fix it, and let me use his truck in the meantime. Sounds sweet, doesn't it? It was. Kind of. Sam was not a very big guy but had a big laugh and deep, confused brown eyes. It didn't take long to notice the pain he held in them. His face and arms were tan and weathered from work, and he had the smile lines of a sixty-year-old at the age of thirty. He kept his arms crossed across his chest in a defensive stance and glared at everything he looked at. Sometimes it was like the sunlight itself was his enemy.

Sam didn't really ask me if he could fix my car. He just told me he was going to take it, and that was that. I instantly liked his take-charge personality, and even though he was acting annoyed with me, I knew that this was his way of being nice. Steve never took charge and fixed things. This was new to me, and I was intrigued.

The weekend after the car incident, my friends took me to a bar at a marina on the river. Daniel was staying with my parents, and I was doing something that I had never done before—going out with friends. I'd had a few wine coolers and we were having a great time dancing and rooting on the karaoke singers belting out Journey. I left the dance floor to head to the bathroom and danced my way around the corner when *wham*! I nearly ran someone right over. I am not the most graceful person on the planet, and I take corners a little short, so I wasn't as surprised as my victim.

"Slow your ass down!"

Wait…I knew that voice.

"Sam! I am so sorry!" I offered to buy him a drink and

we sat down at the bar. He still had his take-charge personality, but this time it wasn't as intriguing, just cocky.

"So what's your story?" Sam asked.

I told him that I had just moved back from Carbondale with Daniel.

"Ohhhh. So you're one of those. Probably left your poor man with nothing and took everything, including the kid, like you little sluts do."

Whoa whoa whoa. I would like to say that at this point I dumped my beer on his head and told him to go to hell, but I didn't. I did, however, stand back, cock my head, and ever so calmly said, "*You* don't know anything about me," then walked away. I could tell Sam felt a little bad, but he slugged back his beer that I bought him and put up two fingers to let the bartender know he was ready for another.

The bars in my hometown close at 3 a.m. This might not seem out of the ordinary for someone who grew up in a city, but for a village with a population of 2,100 that has only one grocery store and it closes at 8 p.m., it seemed a little…well…late.

It was around 2 a.m. now and Sam had pissed me off so badly that I hammered back a few shots. Remember when I said that I had never gone out drinking with my friends? Well, I was (and still am) a lightweight. Through my blurry eyes I saw Sam still sitting alone at the bar, and like a tiger sneaking up slowly on her prey, I approached Sam and poked him hard in the back.

"*You* are a jerk…and…and…" Shit…I was trying to hold back tears but suddenly they were flowing down my face. All of the years of Steve came pouring out of my eyes, and I was doubled over in the ugliest, wine-cooler-plus-shots-induced cry that you have ever seen. Sam stood up fast and grabbed my shoulders.

"Hey, hey, hey…come on now. You're alright," he said. But I wasn't.

The room started to spin and my stomach was flip-flopping and I had black mascara smeared all over my face. Sam took my keys out of my purse, walked me to the door, put me in his truck, and drove me home. I was still wailing like a wounded animal as we crossed the bridge back into town, but Sam didn't say a word except, "Come on."

When we pulled into my driveway, he got me out of the passenger seat and into my house, helped me change my shirt, held me up while I washed my face, and then tucked me into bed. He then turned off my lights, locked my front door, and shut it behind him. He started his truck and went home.

The following Monday I had pulled into the gas station for coffee when I saw Sam's truck pull in behind me. I was a little embarrassed because of how things went down on Saturday, but Sam didn't give me a chance to apologize. In fact, I felt like he hardly even acknowledged me at all. It was like we were two strangers who shared a moment and were now strangers again.

This song and dance would go on for two years. Sam and I would be "strangers" all week long until Thursday "dollar bottle night" came along, and Sam would show up at my door after a night of drinking to kick off the weekend. The weekends now consisted of me chasing Sam from bar to bar and him acting like he didn't care until the sun came up and I would crawl out of his bed. I felt like the only time Sam showed any interest in me was in the dead of night. But that game of cat and mouse had me so intoxicated that not even the country boys sitting on their barstools on Thursday nights could drink it up faster than me.

Remember earlier when I mentioned having a talent for running into the fire and how I said it wasn't just once?

Fire running occasion number two had taken the stage. I want to make a point here, but to be honest, I know that if you are chasing a Sam, then you aren't going to hear me. Someday, though, you will, and you will remember this part and we'll be connected for life. We are the survivors of what I like to call savior syndrome. Savior syndrome is when we know deep down in our heart of hearts that we can bring someone who is in darkness into the light, and they will forever be grateful to us for saving their souls and showing them all the happiness that the world has to offer and give us unconditional love for eternity. All these things would be tied up with a pink satin ribbon in a perfect little bow. Sounds like a fairy tale, right? Well, it is.

Honey, if you think you're going to save him, you aren't. I am sorry to be blunt, but there isn't enough time to be gentle here. The clock is ticking and time is running out. If you are trying to save him you will go under trying, and while he scratches and claws and uses you to push himself up, you will drown. One of the most important lessons I learned from trying to love Sam was that I was also trying to love myself.

Speaking of stages, around the same time I met Sam, I had started going out with my friends quite a bit. Three of my best friends had moved back home after leaving the state and trying to make their relationships work, finding themselves in similar positions as Steve and me. We each suddenly found ourselves single and in our early twenties. My duplex served as makeup, hair, pizza, slumber party, late night party, hangover cure central on the weekends when we didn't have our kids; on weekends when we did have them, we would pile up blankets in the living room and put our money together for boxes of mac and cheese, frozen pizzas, dinosaur chicken nuggets, and the ingredients for fruit pizza. If you've never had fruit pizza, Google it *now*.

Our kids were raised together like siblings. If one of us had to work, the one who didn't took the load of the kids and vice versa. If a drunk ex showed up and tried to take the kids (yes, this happened more than once by more than one ex), we were protectors. If we had a bad date, we were backup emergency plan B. We were warriors for each other. Among the four of us we were working day shifts, night shifts, and going to school; when one of us couldn't go on for one more minute, the other seamlessly picked up right where she left off.

Some of the best times of my life took place during this period. We formed unbreakable bonds that continue to this day. Ladies, these are the kind of women you want in your tribe. They aren't perfect humans, and that's what makes them perfect friends.

My friend Heather and I would tuck three car seats in the back of my car and ride around singing Mary Chapin Carpenter and Trisha Yearwood songs until the kids were asleep. Heather was in nursing school, worked part time at the hospital, and had two kids. Her oldest was a girl who was only one year older than her youngest and Daniel.

Heather liked to sing too, so we would go out and listen to bands together. This was in 2000 and karaoke was just starting to pick up speed, so one night we found ourselves at a bar with karaoke. I had not sung in front of anyone since Hair Brains, but I thought it looked like fun, so I wrote down a title and a number that I got out of a big white binder, and twenty-five minutes later the host called me up. I picked Terri Clark's "You're Easy On The Eyes" and stepped behind the screen. Four hot pink lines disappeared one by one as the intro played.

It was meant to be fun and meaningless, and after three minutes, I hung the mic back on the stand and picked my drink back up, when all of the sudden a sound I had never heard before erupted—cheers and whistling and clapping. What in the heck was going on? Why were we all clapping? Was there a touchdown in the football game on the TVs? Had someone just won a dart competition? Bingo? Oh my God. They were clapping for me. No, no, no! No one was supposed to be actually listening! This was awful. And then I saw Sam, standing in his usual spot, shaking his head and smiling. I wanted to melt into the ground and let someone mop me up. But to be completely honest, after the night was over and Heather and I were lying side by side in my bed watching the fan go around in the silence and recapping the night….. to be absolutely truthful.. it felt amazing, and I couldn't wait to do it again.

I sang a ton of karaoke. No, really, I am telling you, I sang a *ton* of it.

I had also started writing poetry again after a ten-year hiatus, but this time it was more free, open writing and not so rhymey-rhymey. I also adopted a piano from my grandparents' house, and even though my brother absorbed most of the piano lessons (and guitar lessons) from when we were kids, I knew enough piano to put some music to what I was writing.

Late at night after Daniel was fast asleep in his race car bed, I would play a few chords and sing a few words. On the weekends I would go out and find places to sing. I don't always love to admit that I became a karaoke junkie, but when you don't have someone to play the music, you find a way. I learned how to develop tone, pitch, and strength back in those days, and while the rest of the bar was going drink for drink with each other, I was slamming water and trying to see if I could outdo myself.

People started asking me to sing and requested songs. This, of course, made me feel like a rock star, so I was always happy to oblige. Not long after I discovered karaoke, I was asked to sing at friends' weddings and parties. Once in a while a band called Mad Money would play at my favorite little hometown bar, and they would let me get up and sing "Me And Bobby McGee" or The Rolling Stones' "Honky Tonk Women".

I became addicted to the way a microphone smelled and the invisible fence that separated the crowd from the band space. I felt safe there. I still feel safe there, plus with my constant fear of dying, there always seems to be an exit to the side of the stage, and that makes me feel better in general.

Anyway, I spent some months doing things like this as much as possible. Meanwhile, the little chords and words back home were becoming songs, and I had pages of them. Living in a tiny town in North Central Illinois doesn't exactly provide options for music opportunities. I didn't know where to go next, but I knew a friend of the family who had played all his life, so I called him. He suggested putting a demo together so that I could "shop" myself around, and he gave me the name and number of a music studio and producer. I called the number immediately and a nice guy named Rick booked a session for me.

Since I didn't have any of my own songs done, I decided to bring backing tracks to sing to, and since I didn't have many backing tracks, I called the one guy I knew who would…Party Hardy. He ran Party Hardy Karaoke and was the top dog on the karaoke/DJ circuit. He had thousands of songs, and I was able to pick a few that he used to make a CD to take the studio with me.

When it came time to go to the studio, I armed myself with my backing track CD, a couple bottles of water, and enough nerves to make me consider turning my car around.

If you are a musician, I think you will understand what I am about to explain. If you are not, I hope that you have the chance to experience a music studio at least once in your life. My experience at the studio was life-changing. It was almost the same emotion as when I met my hair peeps and knew I had found a home, except this time I was in a setting that was totally foreign yet familiar. I knew I loved it, even before I knew it. Old leather couches hugged the corners of the garage-turned-recording-studio walls. Guitars and percussion instruments hung on hooks on the walls between band posters and a large framed photo of The Beatles' *Abbey Road* album cover. Along the longest wall was a long black and silver control board with two lava lamps on either side bubbling up green gobs of glittery goo that would break off into smaller bubbles in a silent interpretive-style dance.

The control board looked like something that belonged to NASA with its sliders and buttons and lights and knobs. A large rectangular window gave way to another room that housed shiny microphones and rows and rows of black cables wrapped in perfect circles. This room was lined in gray sound panels that made everything sound muffled when you talked. A single pair of earphones was draped over the silver mic, and it looked like a picture from *Rolling Stone* magazine.

Rick took my backing track CD and loaded it into the program he was using to track my songs. He showed me how to adjust the volume on the headphones and had me check the mic a couple of times to get the volume set in his room. The windscreen in front of the mic smelled like new plastic, and the hum of a dehumidifier plus the dimmable lights made the vocal room comfy and relaxed.

"Okay, here we go. Let's see what we can get here," said Rick as the music started in my ear. I missed the mark by a mile.

I heard a click in my ear, and Rick's voice came through the headphones.

"No biggie, let's go again…here we go."

And once again the music started. When I was a little more relaxed, I was able to get a few lines of the first song out before Rick would stop me here and there and say things like, "Here we go…from the chorus" or "One more take of that last line, please, and…here we go."

Finally, after a long session I left with a copy of three songs on a CD. Whenever I listen back to that first demo,

I smile. I should probably cringe because my voice is so inexperienced and green, but I smile because it reminds me of the time when I fought back every unfounded fear, drove my car to a stranger's house, fought every insecurity, knocked on the door, shook his hand, introduced myself, and started what would be the rest of my life.

A few weeks after recording the demo, I sat at my kitchen table and cut slits into a stack of matte black folders. Inside the right pocket was a cringe worthy headshot of me sitting on a stool, holding a guitar. I didn't play much guitar, but I figured if I was going to take a real musician headshot, then I better look like one. In the left pocket was my bio and in the slit in the front of the pocket, my demo. I placed each folder in a manila envelope and hand wrote the address to every single Nashville record label I could find in the yellow pages. Oh, silly girl. I mean, you can't blame me for trying, but I was so green that it makes me shake my head when looking back.

One by one the "thanks but no thanks" letters started rolling in. Every time I would go to my mailbox and see "RCA, Nashville, TN" or "Epic Records, Nashville, TN", I would run into the house, tear open the envelope, and stare blankly at the white crisp piece of paper that once again told me "No."

I know now that this was such a huge part of me growing as an artist. Let's talk for a second about paying your dues. There are many, many musicians who have put years, training, sweat, and blood into learning their craft. There are hundreds of them who have traveled the country for nickels, putting their relationships, stability, and futures on hold. Broken marriages, dependency issues, depression, bankruptcy, dive bars, empty rooms, drunken hecklers, sleazy venue owners, high bar tabs, broken-down equipment trailers, lack of sleep, shitty tavern pizza diets…and for what, you ask? All for "the feeling". The one you get when all of the stars align and a full room of appreciative music-loving people create an energy so forceful that you know that it's something bigger than you, or when you create an energy so big on stage that no words are needed, but everyone on that stage just went to church. To get that prize, you must pay your dues.

I have mixed feelings about the big reality singing shows because I feel that sometimes they are skipping past the stuff that makes a musician a musician. You can take every lesson on the planet and play like no one else, but unless you pay those dues and understand that "the feeling" is actually the same whether you are playing to a full appreciative room or a room with one local drunk, until you understand that it's not about being the center of attention in the spotlight but about stepping outside of yourself and making the audience feel like they are the center of attention, or connecting with no words with a group of people who were once strangers but are now your band family, until you clearly understand that part, then you are not ready. And I was nowhere near ready.

About a month after I started getting letters back from Nashville, I fell back into going out with my friends and took a break from "shopping" myself. Once again we found ourselves in the local bar writing down song titles on little slips of paper and waiting to be called up to sing. The town I grew up in was busy in the summer because a lot of people who lived in Chicago and the suburbs would come down for the weekend and boat on the Illinois River. Because Seneca was nestled right along the riverbanks, we had marinas that lined the shores. Boaters could pull up their boats and dock them, walk up the sand hill, and grab lunch or drinks. There was always some kind of live entertainment happening during the day and usually karaoke at night. It was a fun time of year because the boaters were in vacation mode and they were kicked back enough to join in.

It was late in the evening on a Saturday night. I had gone up and sung a Shania Twain song and a Reba McEntire/Linda Davis duet with Heather when a couple of guys in their thirties approached us. They were both tall and clearly not local. One man was wearing a Harley Davidson shirt and a bandana on his head but didn't look like the guys I knew who rode Harleys because he was too clean cut, and the other had jet-black hair, a perfect jawline, and smiling Irish eyes. They introduced themselves as Andy and George. They were here from the suburbs and were staying on Andy's houseboat at the neighboring marina. Jawline George asked me if I would sing a duet with him, and when I said sure, he picked "Summer Nights" from *Grease*. When we took the stage he was animated, funny, and could, surprisingly, sing.

After we finished our performance and high fived, the guys bought Heather and me a beer and introduced us to their wives, who were sitting at a table and cheering us on. Andy and George then told us that they had a band in the burbs and asked us both if we would be interested in coming out the following week for an audition. At first we thought they were pulling our leg, but their wives assured us that they weren't creepy old guys and that they did have a band, so we made plans to drive up the following Saturday to audition. I was so excited that I could hardly sleep for a week, but Heather remembered she had to work at the hospital that Saturday and couldn't go. I must have asked her a million times if she was *sure* she didn't care if I went without her. She told me to stop thinking of reasons not to go and just go already.

A week later I was navigating my way through White Eagle, a gorgeous and fancy neighborhood that held rows of castle-like houses on one side of the road and perfect green golf course hills on the other. Waiting in the basement for me were the five men who would become my first band. My first set of band boys. Brothers. The keepers of the live music gate.

These guys were what we in the industry call "weekend warriors". They all had heavy-duty careers during the week, and we would practice on weekends in George's finished basement. We didn't have a band name yet but decided that we would be called "Dead Man Drag" after a party trick that one of the guys' friends had perfected.

After a few months of practice and a home demo recording, we booked our first gig. We decided that we needed a dress rehearsal, so we planned a neighborhood kids' birthday party at George's house for a few weeks before the actual show.

The day of the "house" show, I pulled into George's driveway to find fire trucks and an ambulance. Worried sick, I ran into the house to see what the emergency was (relax, there was no smoke…no, I didn't run into a burning house). I heard a commotion coming up the basement stairs and heard George apologizing to the fire chief. Apparently, George decided to buy a smoke machine the morning of the party and hooked it up to test it out, which set off the in-house fire alarm, which then automatically called the fire department. George and his wife, Erin, had already pulled a couch out to their front porch to make room for the band and were getting some dirty looks from the passing neighbors. It was this day that the band gave themselves the nick name "White Trash of White Eagle".

Our first real gig was fast approaching. I invited Sam and Craig, my parents, some coworkers, and a few other family members. The venue was in a strip mall and boasted a large curved stage lined with chicken wire. The bar was smoky and old and reminded me of the tavern that served hamburgers after my dad's softball games when my brother and I were little. The actual bar was raised and could be reached by going up a couple of red-carpeted stairs. High-top tables were scattered throughout the room facing the stage and had high-back maroon vinyl barstools pushed up to them. Each table had a black round plastic ashtray and a table talker with a handwritten sign tucked in that read "PBR Can $1.50 Tenderloin w/ Fries $5.25".

A few TVs on wall mounts towered over the bar and a few older men who were sitting at the bar stared blankly at the Cubs game. The Cubs were losing and the men's faces were twisted in frustration, lighting cigarettes from their soft packs. Once in a while one of the men would pull a red bar chip off the top of a pile with his nicotine-stained fingers and motion to the bartender, who was mixing Bloody Marys, for another can of beer.

A few short hours later we were set up and sound checked and it was showtime. I had worn a tight black mini skirt and a hot pink baggy sweater that fell off the shoulders. I had black boots that hit mid-calf, and even though they were a little small, I liked that they made my legs look long. I still hadn't built up much confidence between Steve and now Sam, so it took me a really long time to pick out an outfit for my first paid show. They say in show biz that you are a professional once you get paid, so I was excited to get my first cut.

A few people had wandered in and the place was finally starting to have some energy. The time had come to take my place on stage. The set list had me in line to sing the first song, "Middle Of The Road" by The Pretenders. The stage lights went on, and Andy started playing the first riff to the first song. I put the mic to my mouth to sing the first line, opened my mouth and… Nothing. Nothing came out. I was totally blank. The words were in my head, but it was like my head and my mouth were suddenly not connected anymore.

The guys all exchanged glances and restarted the song. Once again Andy started the beginning riff, and as I was about to try to sing the first line again an older lady yelled from the bar, "You suck!"

People…this was my first experience on stage with a live band. No sparkly *American Idol* sequined dress, no flashy stage with footlights and glitter, no built-in audience cheering my name. Nope. Just me, the lady from the bar who hated me, some chicken wire, and a whole lotta paying dues ahead.

This is such an interesting time for me to look back on. Had I quit here because of a person who felt the need to make another person feel small, I wouldn't have had any of the people or experiences in my life that I have had. Someone could argue that I wouldn't know any different, but I truly think I would still be soul searching. Be brave, friends. Take chances. Go ahead and do it. Fail a few times.

I had a discussion with Terry this morning about failure. My take on it is this—if you have something burning in the deepest part of your belly, then the only way to fail is if you don't take action. You might open that bakery or start your line of handmade cosmetics and it might not work at first. Are you a failure? No, you are not. But why, you ask? If you try something and it doesn't work, that is failing, right? *No!* If it doesn't work, then it means one thing: it needs tweaking.

No one ever said that being brave means you instantly succeed the moment you decide to follow your authenticity. It takes a lot of hard work, learning, redoing, retrying, and reinventing yourself. It will cost you tears, stress, and in my case, a new and constant symptom of heart palpitations…but the only way you fail is if you don't do it. Read that again. The *only* way you can fail is if you *don't* do it.

Once you take that first step, one of two things will happen:

(1) You get brave, you take the first step, and it works. You find yourself living a new version of your old self. One who loves going to work, school, or home. One who feels the warmth of the fire in a place that used to be cold.

(2) You get brave, you take the first step, and it doesn't work, but it's too late…you've already been given a glimpse of the new version of you. You've already felt the flicker of the fire and now you're determined to make it roar. You learn the lessons that are needed to move to the next step

of your journey, the ones that will ultimately lead you to number one above. As soon as you adapt to this new way of thinking, you will be unstoppable because you'll realize that the only way you fail yourself is if you don't do it.

Sam didn't show up for my first show. I think he thought it was dumb that I was driving all the way up to the suburbs to play onstage with guys I hardly knew. I also think he was sure that all they wanted was to get me in bed, and as dysfunctional of a relationship as we had, he did play a protective role in my life.

It took me a long time to realize that Sam actually did care about me, and in his very backward way of understanding, I think he showed me love as much as he knew how.

Dead Man Drag was starting to book more shows, so we changed the band's name to AKA after a while because Dead Man Drag just seemed a little hard to book at graduation parties and weddings. "Who's playing your engagement party?" "Oh, Dead Man Drag." It just didn't work. So we were now AKA.

I developed lifelong friendships over the few years that I played with these guys. It was a fun time in my life because I was still in my early twenties and technically single other than my confusing friendship with Sam. Truthfully, I had no interest in dating at all. The few times when I did go on the obligatory date, it usually resulted in me making some sort of excuse to go home early. I was really kind of a drag in that department. I never really fit in well with anyone at that point in my life, and that made it hard to connect.

One year in the middle of summer, Craig's brother was getting married. Craig, Sam, and I were like three peas in a pod and did most things together, so I had just assumed that we would all go together. Craig was in the wedding, so again I assumed that I would just be attending with Sam, but a few weeks earlier I had noticed a change in him that had me on edge. The Thursday dollar bottle night phone calls had lessened and his truck wasn't in town as much.

Sam and I had an agreement early on that if one of us met someone who we thought we would like to date, we would be honest with the other about it. It's the kind of deal you agree to when you are twenty-two and insecure. Anything for his attention. So I shouldn't have been surprised when Sam told me that he was going to be taking another girl to the wedding but that I could still ride with them.

You guys...I was so pathetic at this time of my life that I actually rode to the wedding with them. I went to the bar for pre-drinks and sat right across from them, danced with Sam at the wedding once, and then watched him dance with her the rest of the night and stopped by yet another bar for a post-wedding drink with...yep, you guessed it... both of them.

By that time of night I had so much physical pain in my chest from being the third wheel and so much champagne in me that this third wheel was about to fall off and bounce down the highway like an out-of-control tire that has flown off of a semitruck. So there we were, the three best friends that anyone could have (nod to the hangover, because I was about to have a good one).

Walking into a little river marina bar at midnight, I almost felt bad for Sam at this point. *Almost.* The other girl couldn't figure out why I was still with them, and I couldn't figure out why other girl was still cramping my style. He was sort of in the middle of what seemed like a good idea but was starting to go south really fast.

So close your eyes and picture this. Get comfortable because things are about to get really cringy. Go ahead, I'll wait. Ready? There was a band playing on the stage and a few drunken patrons dancing in bikini tops, cutoff shorts, and no shoes.

I was in a black glitter floor-length dress with heels that put me well over 5'11, and I was downing shots of Irish whiskey. I slammed down the last shot glass and strutted—

and I mean *strutted*—up to the stage like I was on one of the runways back in my modeling days. In my mind, I imagined it looked like long, sexy strides. One foot in front of the other with a little cross action at the knee. Shoulders back, head up, and pouring out a little half smile that looked confident and determined. What I think I *actually* looked like in reality was a mix between someone who had to poop and someone who had Bell's palsy. Or maybe someone who had Bell's palsy who had to poop. Yeah, that's it.

So I strutted up to the band and I asked them if I could sing one. Side note: professional musicians should never ever *ask* to be a guest on stage. If we are invited and accept, then that is okay, but never, ever ask. So I was at cringe level five out of ten at that point. Oh, but wait, it gets worse.

They said sure, I could sing a song.

I learned something that night about myself. I can't sing when I've been drinking. I mean, I have a ton of stage personality and can rock a high kick, but somewhere along the shot line I just lose my rhythm, pitch, and technique. All pretty darn important qualities of a singer. So Ms. Champagne Meets Irish Whiskey was now on stage with a live mic in her hand. You're closing your eyes right now because you know what's about to go down, don't you?

I dedicated my performance to "Sam and his new girlfriend" and belted out the worst version of "Me And Bobby McGee" that you've ever heard. In between words I took the liberty of ad-libbing a few vulgar comments directed toward Sam and fake-laughed my way through the solo. Oh God. It makes my stomach hurt even just writing about it now.

I finished my amazing performance with a mic drop. Please, please, if you have made it this far with me, listen closely. Don't ever drop someone's mic. They are expensive and they are not yours to drop. It doesn't make the feedback sound when you do it like in the commercial anyway, so all you're left with is a really nonthreatening thump. Also, don't swear in someone's mic. If you're ever all pissed off and drinking Irish whiskey, you'll thank me for this information. You're welcome.

So I dropped the mic. The drunk ladies with no shoes told me that I was amazing (I was not), and Sam was livid. I had embarrassed myself, I had embarrassed him, and the other girl was just staring in disbelief. Sam told me that the train was leaving and if I wanted a ride home, I had better get in. I threw a fit. I wouldn't get in. She was in the front. I would just walk the sixteen miles home. At 1 a.m. In the middle of nowhere.

Sam should have let me, but he damn near hog wrestled me into his back seat and child locked me in. I reverted back to the terrible twos, and I was literally pushing the back of her seat with my knees. For the whole long sixteen miles.

Once in my driveway I wouldn't get out. "Let's take her home and then come back to my house," I suggested. There was a standoff in my driveway and finally, after a very long twenty minutes, I gave up. She won. I got out of the car, slammed the door so hard the windows shook, ugly cried up my stairs while he tried to unlock my door and get me in, and hung on his neck begging, crying, trying not to gag, for him to please bring her home and come back.

He didn't come back. In fact, he didn't even call.

As if this wasn't enough to have to deal with on Sunday morning, aside from waking up to the feeling of heavy pounding in my head, I suddenly had the vivid realization that this was the last day my memere and pepere would live in the house he built from the ground up. Pepere's health had started to decline, so they were at the point in life that it was time to move into a duplex with less to take care of. I had previously asked Sam to come and help move a few things with his truck on Monday, but I figured after my incredible show of grace and respect, he would most likely not show up.

Oh, but he did show up, and the second I saw him all of my hurt and anger returned.

Luckily, there was another guy pulling in with a truck that was an acquaintance of some of my family. I didn't know him very well. He was eleven years older than me and I only remembered him from a turtle stew cook-off a long, long time ago. I'm not giving him a name in this book because I don't want to breathe life back to this situation, and I just don't know if it's safe to do so. That being said, here's what happened next.

He said hello to me and I noticed Sam was watching.

So I turned on my best flirtatious smile and stepped in a little closer to see if I could make Sam feel a fraction of what I felt on Saturday. Sometimes we are so blinded by our commitment to get even with someone that we don't even see the vulture that is circling, waiting for the right time to swoop in and fly away with his prey. In other words, this was the beginning of my very own personal hell that lasted for a very long time.

I won't bore you with the mundane details, but basically I was sucked in by the undertow before I even knew it.

It started with one lunch and went on to him spoiling me absolutely rotten. Gifts, dinners, weekend getaways, which quickly turned into me moving some of my stuff into his house because he thought it would be a good idea for me to be closer to work and to Daniel's daycare. That quickly turned into him telling me how to spend my money (mind you, I was still working a full forty hours plus at this time) and controlling nearly everything I did.

One night while meeting friends out for drinks, a band called The Clients was playing. He liked to show me off to his buddies, so he flashed the bass player a $50 bill and asked him to get his girlfriend up to sing one. I took the stage and sang "Me And Bobby McGee" with the band, but when I finished, instead of being happy that his $50 got him his way, he was standing at the back of the room, toothpick in his mouth, arms crossed, and clearly irritated.

When I stepped off the stage, he grabbed me by the arm, walked me out to his truck, and told me that we were going home. I begged him to tell me what I did wrong, but the only thing he muttered was that it would be the last time I sang in public unless it was at church. He was mortified that his girlfriend was such an attention seeker, and now looking back, I realize that he liked to keep my light dim, and when I'm on stage it is bright (because when you are doing what you are meant to do you become a blinding light that no one can dim).

He screwed with me so hardcore and did things I look back on and pray no one else has fallen victim to. He was not gentle and held me down on more than one occasion but then backed himself up with apologies and pleas that he thought I liked it.

One time during a dinner out he told me that his life plan included a wife *and* a girlfriend but that he loved me enough to let me be the first to choose which one I wanted to be. Then when I became visibly upset in the restaurant and threatened to leave him there, he started laughing and telling me that I was so gullible and he couldn't believe I fell for that.

He offered to give me an apology gift. A bull ring. I was so young and naive and didn't know what that was. He assured me that it was a nice piece of jewelry, and I actually felt special, ya'll. Later when I told a friend about the wife/girlfriend joke and then explained that everything was okay because "I am just so easy to mess with" and that he was going to give me a special piece of jewelry called a bull ring, she just sat and stared at me in confusion and disbelief. That was when she told me that a bull ring is the metal hoop they put through a cow's nose and hook a rope to in order to lead them around.

I started going home more. I missed my duplex and my space and truthfully, he was starting to make me cringe, so I began to pull away. That was when things started to get terrifying. A few times while driving past the same place, he would point out a wooded area and say, "That's my tree." When I asked him what that meant, he told me that his tree was what he would run us both into if I ever tried to leave. I knew at this point that I had to be smart and take my time to plan my escape.

No one other than Heather really knew yet just how bad it was. Heather saw firsthand the demonic shit he would do, and she was afraid of him. She pleaded and begged me to leave, and I assured her that I was trying. She called me from work to tell me that a coworker had been going on lunch dates with him, and I thought this might be my way out, but in true narcissistic style, he wiggled his way out by making me feel ridiculously insecure and stupid for even thinking that. He said, "How would I have time?"

Meanwhile, Sam was dating the other girl and we hadn't talked at all since moving day. I had considered calling him and asking for his help since he was a police officer, but my pride wouldn't let me, so I didn't.

The final straw came just a few weeks after the bull ring incident, and it was enough to finally help me leave. I was afraid to go home so I packed Daniel up and we called the one person I knew could hide me. George.

I called him while in my car and he told me to come straight to their house and not go home first. He also told me that he had an out-of-town guest staying, but there was plenty of room. I've got another spoiler alert here for you, but I might as well tell you now.

His out-of-town guest ended up being my first husband.

Cue dramatic music here.

Charlie was standing on the front steps of George's home smoking a cigarette when I pulled in. Mascara and tears were dried all over my face from crying over the disbelief that I had allowed myself to get into a situation I'd quickly lost control of. How dumb was I? I mean, I had a three-year-old to think about who was currently sound asleep in the car seat.

Charlie was tall and handsome and had long blond hair that hit his shoulders. He was wearing a black turtleneck sweater, jeans, bare feet, and a small hoop earring in his left ear. He didn't look like the guys I knew from home. No work boots, no camouflage, no trucker-style baseball hat with a feed or tractor company logo on the front.

I feel like I need to pause here for a second. You're probably reading this book seeking inspiration to live your authentic self; it was, after all, filed in the "inspirational" category. So why am I not giving you anything to work with while reading the previous few paragraphs? It's really a simple answer. At this point in my life I was so lost that you would not want to take *any* advice from this girl. But the lessons lie within.

I am sharing each and every part of my life with you—especially these years—so that you can understand that life isn't always good. It isn't always inspirational. I wasn't always in a place where I felt I could help someone. I was the one who needed the person I am today. I want you to really understand this because even if you are lost and broken and you can't see one tiny bit of light, even if you know me and you only know the person I am now and you have assumed that I have always just had it together, I want you to know that you can be the best version of yourself, even if you can't see it yet. Because I couldn't see it in myself yet either.

Charlie offered to help me get Daniel inside. I was too exhausted to argue, so I let him carry the duffle bag that I had shoved everything into. George and Erin showed me to one of their girls' rooms where I could stay for as long as I needed. I laid Daniel down for the night and met George and Charlie back on the front porch. It was late into the night by now, and the guys were in a deep conversation about the pros and cons of using tape vs digital in the recording studio.

I learned that Charlie was in town from Connecticut to write some songs with George. They had been in a band together back east, and Charlie had taken a year off of work to record his album. He had flown in from NYC to Chicago for a break and to find some inspiration.

I was instantly intrigued by Charlie. He was funny and charming and talked a lot about being a musician. His opinions on current music were strong but made him seem smart and passionate. We three stayed up talking about music and art and what led me to George's until the dawn started to peek its pink rays through the darkness.

We went our separate ways to bed, but even for being up all night and having gone through such a dramatic evening, I was surprisingly refreshed. I had never known someone else who understood the passion of writing, and Charlie made it so clear that he could help me with his vast knowledge of being an artist. As we went our separate ways that night, Charlie stopped me and told me that it wasn't really his business but that I shouldn't let someone treat me the way I was being treated. "For what it's worth, I think you're worth way more than that," he said.

Chapter 5
Unloaded

CHARLIE AND I BECAME INSTANT pals. Our long-distance friendship was just what I needed to move on, but I was still dealing with all kinds of crazy on this end of the country. After I asked many times not to be contacted by wife/girlfriend guy (at this point, for the sake of clarity, let's call him WG), things started to get out of hand.

Sam and I had finally talked on 9/11 after the Twin Towers came down and everyone in the country was coming together. I felt the deep need to make amends with Sam, and after that, we were in a good place. He and the other girl had broken up, and he was pretty upset over it. We had both grown some over the past few months, and we had an unspoken understanding that we would always be there for each other as friends.

Sam patrolled on his midnight shift and would call

once in a while in the wee hours of the morning to alert me to WG's truck parked outside my house.

Flowers would show up at work, and the phone calls never seemed to stop. I was getting nervous and constantly looking over my shoulder. Narcissists don't like rejection and will not stop until you're under their thumb again.

One sunny afternoon I walked out to my car at work to go grab some lunch. The office I worked at was out in the country, so no one ever locked their doors. When I opened my driver's side door, there was a stack of papers. Twelve, to be exact. Twelve handwritten pages from WG telling me that he talked to God. By our tree. He went and sat by our tree and talked to God, and God told him that we were meant to be together and that we would be soon. On Earth or in heaven…whatever came first.

I stood there, shaken to my core. Was I reading what I thought I was? Was this a threat? A fear tactic? Was he going to drive us into his tree? *Together on Earth or in heaven.* The most terrifying six words I've ever read.

That was the day I finally went to the police. A few days later, I had a two-year order of protection that WG broke a few times, but finally, after not even a year of living in fear, he left me alone. It took me much longer to get my freedom back; I looked over my shoulder for years.

I am passionate about this topic. In my opinion there are just not enough laws that protect us when someone is stalking, threatening, or scaring another individual. It should be our right to walk into the grocery store without wondering if there is something awful lurking around the corner. It should be everyone's right to have a safe space to live.

If you feel afraid because of another person, please, please, please use this as your reason to call and tell someone. Make them hear you. Do not under any circumstances downplay the issue or feel that you have to justify your reasons.

I'm choosing not to write too much more about WG because I don't think he deserves a whole chapter. If I give that much life to his character, then I feel like I've given life back to an awful situation. I have grown and healed so much since this time in my life, but I felt it necessary to talk about because (1) it shaped who I am today; (2) it's important for others to know there is a way out and a way to gain your own safe space back; and (3) it leads me into the first song I wrote that made an impact.

"Not Your Doll" is one of the first singles I wrote that would eventually go on my first album. WG liked to call me "doll". Ironic, eh?

"Not Your Doll" came on the heels of the order of protection. I was healed enough to write about it but still pissed off enough to want to speak out. I was frustrated with myself for allowing another person to gain control of my emotions, so I took to the pen. Every night after grabbing Daniel from Anne and Bills on my way home from work, I sat down and wrote lyrics, then scratched them out and rewrote them until I felt like they made enough sense. I was still only able to play a few chords on my piano, but it was enough to finish the song.

This wasn't my best song by far, but it was meaningful and sent a message, so I was pretty proud of it. I kept it in my lyric book and tucked it under my bed. I just wasn't sure what the next step would be, so I let go and let God provide that answer.

That answer's name was Bobby Scumaci.

I met Bobby one night after one of the guys in my band told me about an open mic-style jam on Tuesday nights in Naperville. For those of you who aren't familiar with music, let me paint you a picture. Typically an open mic or a jam night is a bunch of musicians who get together and form a house band for the night. Then other musicians can sign up and get up with the band and play and or sing, kind of like an interchange of musicians, if you will. Keep in mind that I don't play any instruments, and at this point I barely knew anything about the music industry.

I walked in, signed up, and waited and watched. The musicians playing were top notch. These were the guys who were off the road from touring and were just having a good time. I wasn't in their league. This was *not* karaoke. This was not the P.C. Lounge or George's basement. I was in an absolute panic, and I was about to try to sneak out the back door…and then I heard my name.

A very burly, good-looking Italian guy called my name off the list while standing behind a keyboard. I quickly walked up to the stage with the entire house band looking at me, waiting for me to tell them what we would play. I turned bright red and barely muttered, "'Bobby McGee' or 'Son of a Preacher Man'."

The good-looking Italian guy asked me what key I sang those in.

Uh…how about the key of I have no idea what I'm doing and everyone is staring at me, so whatever makes me look like maybe I know what I'm doing for a few minutes and then I can get the hell out of here sounds good.

But the guys could tell that I was a nervous wreck, so they taught me. You guys, they stopped what they were doing and with gentle ways and twinkles in their eyes (or maybe it was whiskey and marijuana), these super-pro musicians walked me through the experience and they taught me. Such priceless memories.

After I sang my two songs, the band took a break. The good-looking Italian guy slid next to me in my booth and introduced himself as Bobby Scumaci. His brothers owned the venue and he was just off the road himself from a few years of touring with Dave Mason. He was kind and sweet, and I was instantly in awe of his incredible skill as a musician and his general human kindness. I also liked that he was already sort of protective of me in a sibling way because he knew I was alone and he knew I was totally green.

After the house band went back up, I stayed and listened to the other musicians come up one by one, purely and completely happy. These people were singers, songwriters, and players, and they were opening a secret door to a whole underground world I didn't know existed. An underground land filled with my people! I was surrounded by these talented musicians who had soul and energy, and my life was transformed. I was in love. So I went back the next week.

Bobby seemed genuinely happy to see me and waved me over. After we chatted a while, he told me he had a recording studio and would love to have me come in and sing a couple of tunes that one of the cocktail waitresses wrote. It was like Christmas morning. I could hardly keep from bouncing up and down, but I tried to play it cool and gave him a simple, "Sure, that would be okay."

We set a date and I drove to his studio a few weeks later. This was only my second time being in a recording studio, but the sights and sounds were familiar once again.

Bobby played a couple of demos for me and we got to work. I laid down two versions of the songs, and we decided to sleep on it and listen again the next day. When I came back the next day, we both just kind of knew my voice wasn't right for the songs. They needed something I couldn't give them, so we just left them alone. I wanted to tell Bobby about the songs I had been writing, but in my eyes, I was in no way, shape, or form a songwriter yet, and I didn't want to sound pretentious—I was fine with being a rookie and taking it all in. But I decided to at least let him know, in case he might have an idea of what I should do with my songs.

I probably prefaced my statement with an apology for being forward (I used to apologize a lot for things I shouldn't have, and we'll talk about that soon), but I told him that I had a few songs of my own.

"Okay, cool, J. Bring them in and let's see what we can do," he said.

Whew. Well, that was easy.

J was what almost all of my musician friends called me back then. I think it was just easier for them to remember one letter instead of my whole name. Plus, musicians are just kind of cool like that, giving people nicknames and helping to create new identities for those trying to recreate themselves.

You're probably wondering what happened to Ed. He

was really there for me when I was still living in Carbondale, and I don't want you to think I just blew him off once I moved. He was busy chasing his dream sports career and I was busy chasing my dream music career. Most of the time we would connect on a Sunday via phone after a long weekend and catch up. Other times he would drive to Illinois on his way to a competition or work event, and we would get to spend some much needed time together. Always too short but always the light of my life. I loved having a friend who was working as hard as I was to really do something special with what he loved.

We motivated each other, though neither of us had much at this point. He was working when he could in between winning competitions that would launch him up to the next rank. I was still learning my industry but couldn't stop talking about it, and Ed loved to listen. He would ask me over and over to write him songs. My music was as important to him as it was me. In a world that was so uncertain, it was nice to have a friend who was undoubtedly always there at the end of a crazy week.

Once in a while he would tell me about someone he had gone on a date or two with, but he usually chased them off with his intense focus on his career and this pesky bestie in Illinois who just happened to be a girl. I was part of the package. If they didn't accept me, he didn't date them. My loves, that made me feel like a million bucks.

Looking back, I can't believe I was so blinded by his dedication to me that I didn't see the forest for the trees. I took for granted the fact that Ed would always be with me on my journey. All too soon, reality would slap me in the face. But for now, at this point in the book, he was still part of my song. In fact, if I am being completely truthful, he was my entire song. I just couldn't hear the melody.

A few weeks after bringing Bobby some of my songs he told me that he thought I actually had a really good album ready to record. I was tingling with excitement and honored that someone of his musical caliber would think that my songs were good enough to spend time on. Remember, I'm still really struggling with worth at this point. Hell, I still struggle with it sometimes now.

It wasn't going to be cheap to record an album. There's a lot that goes into it, and it takes time and funds. I had some time, but that was really it.

I turned to the two people who I knew supported my goals: my parents. I asked them for a loan, and my dad told me that we could make it happen now and figure out how I could pay them back later. That was always my parents' trick to making me feel like I wasn't asking for a handout.

Once we started on the first steps to recording the album, everything went really fast. We needed players, and Bobby had a pocket full of players he could call. I was nervous because I didn't think anyone with any kind of experience would want to play for the album, but to my humble surprise I got some of the best players in the Chicago area and a smokin' drummer from Nashville. Not only did they agree to bring my songs to life but they were excited to do it. I can't even begin to describe what it feels like when someone who is seasoned and professional tells you that you are a good writer. *All* the feels.

Charlie and I had started to take our friendship to the next level and had been traveling between Illinois and New York for a while. I fell in love with his family. He had a large

Polish East Coast family that consisted of four brothers, one sister, and the matriarch of the family, their mother. They were cheerfully loud and loving and as smart as a whip. They were creative, educated, and interesting, with a few writers, an entrepreneur, a high-powered executive, and a musician. Charlie was the baby of the family by a good handful of years, and his siblings adored him. The siblings' spouses were equally great and had come from all kinds of backgrounds.

I had never been to New York City or anywhere on the East Coast, and their New York accent and word usage was exciting and fun to me. They used words like "deli" instead of sandwiches and "bananas" instead of crazy. They pronounced Florida "Flahrida" and pronounced coffee like "Cawfee".

They took holidays as a family in the Pocono Mountains, and it was nothing for his mother, who was already in her 70s, to drive into Brooklyn or Manhattan to pick up a few things, a feat that I still have not attempted after my first experience with New York traffic damn near scared the life out of me. New York City was night and day to this Midwestern girl. I loved the pulse and felt swept away by the energy every time I landed at LaGuardia, but it was also overwhelming.

To me, New Yorkers were blunt and independent and knew how to elbow their way around the Big Apple. They could hail a cab in a pair of heels and look like a million bucks getting in. I was in awe of their strong personalities and their love of their city. New York, after all, is the best city in the US, according to every single New Yorker I've met. They love their baseball and have a sharply divided dedication to either the Yankees or the Mets. I love their bagels, pizza, constantly honking horns, and a buzz that you can only describe once you've stood in Times Square.

After months of paying for travel and being tired of long-distance dating, we decided it would make more sense if we lived in the same area, so Charlie decided to move to Illinois.

I sold my duplex that I loved so much, loaded up a U-Haul, and moved once again. Daniel was four now. I was still working at the transportation company and recording my album, but we decided I would move because I couldn't stomach moving Charlie to my tiny Midwestern hometown from a metropolitan area such as NYC. He would have had culture shock, and I would have had culture shock if we moved to Chicago, so we picked a place in the middle. The place where we met: Naperville.

I had a hard time leaving my duplex. In fact, even after it was empty but before it was sold, my friends and I would unlock the door and lay on the living room carpet and reminisce about all of the good memories and hard times we had there. Leaving that duplex was like saying goodbye to an era, and I wasn't exactly comfortable with it, but I think you have to be uncomfortable in order to grow.

Pushing our limits and going where there is pressure is what forces us to grow. If we stay comfortable, we stay right where we are. Yes, we are comfortable, but that can get weary after a while.

I flew out east to attend Charlie's going away party, and after it was over, I flew back home with his cat, and he was going to drive out over the course of a couple of days with the rest of whatever fit in his car.

I had already moved into the Naperville apartment and was getting settled. He wasn't bringing much. Looking back, I sometimes wonder if this should have been my first sign that something was a little off. Charlie was eleven years older than me and I had more to my name than he did. Yes, he had a nice condo, but I never really thought to ask where the furniture inside was going to go. I was just happy to be moving into a new stage of life. My hometown represented Sam and all that went down the last few years, so it was time to go. This was what I kept telling myself even though my heart pulled back a little. Still, I ignored it.

Charlie was supposed to leave and arrive two days later. He was going to stop and see a friend in Ohio, then continue on to Illinois. After three days of him not answering his phone, I started to worry that something had happened. On the fourth day, when he finally called to tell me that he would be in Illinois the next day, I was confused. He didn't seem sorry but only explained that his friend was going through some things and needed him. He would get to me soon.

I guess I was thinking he would be more excited to start our new life together and wouldn't be able to get to Illinois fast enough, but something was off. Still, I ignored it.

Charlie finally arrived and we began our lives together. He found a job as a technical writer for a headhunting corporation and I continued to work at my job in transportation. I still cut hair on the side and had found a part-time gig at a JCPenney salon. Shoutout to those JCP salons, with me every step of the way! I was still recording my album while we were falling into our new groove.

Steve was still finishing school and only saw Daniel

a handful of times throughout his young life, so Charlie stepped in, and when Steve graduated from college and moved back, we had a transitional period but eventually got used to Daniel going every other weekend to see his dad.

I've thought long and hard about how to write what happened next. To be honest, I'm still not exactly sure when the decline began, but I do know it wasn't long after Charlie arrived. I'm going to be as transparent as I can while remaining respectful so that I cause as little hurt as possible. I do want to say that we had some great years. We did love each other, or at least the idea of each other, but things were changing. And they were changing fast.

I don't regret marrying Charlie. We had a beautiful wedding with an incredible reception filled with friends and family from all over the country, but what I would like for you to know is how rocky things were before we even said, "I do." No one really knew. I was hearing a faint whisper from a familiar voice. Like a strong older sister who knows how to speak up when you're going to get yourself into trouble, I had my own personal security system—my gut. But I would shush her with thoughts like, "Every relationship is going to have trials," and sometimes I would just flat out tell her to shut up. And when she seemed to get even louder, I would unplug her completely and shove her away in a corner. Like a blender the day after Cinco de Mayo.

Why did I push away my gut instincts, you might be asking? It's okay, I've asked myself a million times. My answer is simple. Three words. Disappointment. Pride. Fear.

Disappointment

As you've learned, I had some really crappy situations in the span of just a few years. My parents did things like driving a U-Haul to Carbondale a few weeks after I left so that I could have the rest of my stuff, babysitting for Daniel on nights when I went out with friends or to the studio, deep cleaning my duplex only a few short years after buying it for me to rent, helping me pack up my duplex and move into the Naperville apartment. This doesn't even begin to describe the situations my parents cleaned up for me as I moved along like a small tornado.

So how could I possibly tell them that I had once again made a mistake? Not to mention the fact that Charlie left a life on the East Coast to live with me, and it wasn't exactly the easiest transition. It wasn't like he lived in the next town over and could just go back. Anyway, what would his family think? They seemed to be so overjoyed that Charlie had found his way to the Midwest, almost breathing a sigh of relief. At the time, I didn't know this but his family had been worried about him and thought it would be a good move for him to make and find a place to start fresh. I would understand this much better after the dust settled.

Pride

Charlie and I were the perfect example of love. At one point while still long-distance dating, we even made ourselves sick being so lovey-dovey. We were in love with the idea of being in love. We were both creative singer-songwriters, so we believed in fairy-tale storybook endings. Our friends were so happy for us, even though some of my friends started to see through it. How could I tell them the truth? That things weren't perfect. That after all the talking up I did, maybe our relationship wasn't so great after all.

Have you ever gone to a restaurant and had an absolutely perfect experience, so you tell all of your friends and family about it and they want to go try it for themselves, so you all go back but this time things aren't as good? You've spent all this time talking up your experience, relationship, job, whatever, and now you're panicking inside a little because you don't want your pride to take a hit, and if I were to admit that I was wrong, that maybe things weren't as great as I was leading everyone to believe, my pride definitely would have been hurt.

Fear

Fear was the biggest out of all of the above. Fear that I was never going to find love. Fear that this was real life and maybe things couldn't be a fairy-tale storybook. Fear that I was never going to find what I truly desired and would be making a mistake by continuing my search. Maybe I was just never happy and impossible to please. Maybe I had set my expectations too high and what I imagined, craved, and hoped for was not attainable. All of this work to get settled into a new start, and yet I wasn't settled. Fear that I would walk into the fire yet again. I mean, he didn't dump things on me, pretend he didn't know me, or threaten to drive me into trees, so maybe this *was* a good thing, and maybe I was just too selfish to notice. So. Much. Fear.

If you are feeling this, give me a *yes, girl, yes*! All too often we continue on with something that isn't healthy or meant for us because we are afraid to disappoint or afraid our pride will be blemished. What we must understand is that if we don't listen to our inner voice now, then eventually it will be so loud that we won't have any choice but to hear it, and by that time days, months, years, or decades could have gone by, and *that* is really the only thing we should fear.

Charlie and I moved closer to my family a month after we got married. Our apartment was getting to be too expensive and we needed a school that offered full-time kindergarten for Daniel. Plus, our time in Naperville just felt like it was coming to an end. So we packed up and moved into a cute little duplex in a quiet neighborhood.

The neighbors were mostly young couples with young children, so we felt comfortable right away. We almost immediately became close with our neighbors across the street, Andrea and Johnny. These two amazing people would become such a cornerstone in my life that it was without a doubt no mistake and absolutely divinely intended that we moved in across from them.

Charlie was still driving to the suburbs to work and I was still with the transportation company. Around this time, I had started to market the album. Bobby and I finished it, and our first delivery of perfectly packaged CDs arrived a few weeks after moving in. Just as I did with the first demo, I sat at my desk and sent off press packages to record label execs. Google was a thing now, so that made it easier to find contacts, and with the rise of online music it also made it easier to get your name and your songs in front of a larger audience.

Through a friend in the radio business, I had been introduced to an online distribution company called DSN. DSN featured artists and distributed music to radio stations all over the world, including syndicated stations and online stations. I sent a few singles over for DSN to review, and to my surprise, they offered me a five-year distribution deal. Soon, "Not Your Doll", the first single off of the album that we titled *Listen*, was featured on the DSN website and available for download worldwide.

A few weeks later, DSN started sending me weekly updates that included different countries around the world and the number of downloads from each country. Soon after that, I was recognized as the top downloaded artist for DSN, bringing in over 250,000 downloads of "Not Your Doll". It was surreal and unfortunately just on the brink of iTunes, so most of the downloads were free downloads, but it was about getting my name out there and ultimately telling my story through music, never about the money.

Not long after the recognition from DSN, another music colleague told me about a competition called Next American Superstar, where female recording artists from all over the USA submitted their original songs for a chance to travel to Dallas, TX and perform at the world famous Gilley's with the potential to be named the Next American Superstar.

Ironically the competition worked hand in hand with trucking companies and SiriusXM Radio. Each contestant would be sponsored by a large national trucking company and would be required to do some radio spots along with performances in exchange for promotional materials like posters and travel expenses for touring.

I was somehow lucky enough to make the top six, and before I knew it I was sponsored by US Xpress. I had a couple of months before I would get on a plane and head to Dallas, but sometime during those months I felt a strange yet all too familiar twinge in my lower right side.

I tried to ignore it. I tried to pretend it wasn't there, but after a week of not feeling well and throwing up every day from the pain, I knew it couldn't wait any longer. So I made an appointment, and a few hours later I was staring at a small black circle on an ultrasound screen while the ultrasound tech desperately looked for a heartbeat.

I was pregnant. But something was very wrong.

Charlie was coming home later and later from work, and when he did finally get home, something just wasn't right. I knew it wasn't another woman, or at least I assumed so because it wasn't just his personality, it was his physical self—his walk, his talk, his movements. Something was off, but I didn't know what. When I would ask him if something was wrong or if he was feeling okay, he would just reassure me that he was totally fine and normal. And then he would ask me if I was okay in a worried tone that made me ask myself if I actually was okay.

A few hours after the ultrasound came the bloodwork, which was then repeated forty-eight hours later to see if my HCG (pregnancy hormone) had risen. In a healthy pregnancy, HCG levels will double every seventy-two hours. Mine were plummeting, and my doctor still couldn't find a heartbeat a few days later at a second ultrasound.

We scheduled one more ultrasound in the hope that

maybe we were just too early and it wasn't detectable yet, but my doctor, who was more like a father figure to me at this point, prepared me for the worst.

Nonviable fetus, natural miscarriage, D&C—these were all terms flying around my head. Terms that instead should have been healthy fetus, thriving heartbeat, nice strong numbers. To make matters worse, I had to walk around not knowing if there was a viable or nonviable fetus in my belly. Grabbing milk at the grocery store became a game of keeping my head down so that I didn't accidentally make eye contact with a mom pushing a cart with an infant or a toddler in the seat, in fear of becoming an instant puddle of tears.

I kept high hopes that we were just too early, and I caressed and talked to my flat stomach with encouraging words like a Little League coach. "We've got this…come on, kiddo…you're okay. Keep fighting. Stay in it, I'm rooting for you. I know you're strong…you have *got* this." But a few days later, we lost the game.

On a clear, sunny summer Friday morning, my doctor and I decided to schedule a D&C for the following Tuesday if I didn't miscarry naturally over the weekend. A third ultrasound had revealed my worst fear to be true. Still no heartbeat. This was officially a nonviable fetus. An "unsustained pregnancy" in medical terms, but to me they were telling me that my baby had died. Things went pretty fast after we were out of limbo. The weekend came and went, and Monday morning I met with the anesthesiologist, followed by lunch at Memere's. She made me the most amazing lunch. Escargot oozing with bubbling salty garlic butter served with warm crusty French bread to sop up all of the deliciousness, butter lettuce dressed lightly in a Dijon and shallot vinaigrette, steak frites (only the very best pan-fried steak with hand-cut and baked French fries). For dessert there was homemade French apple custard pie, an open-faced, delicate, flaky pastry crust filled with perfectly layered thinly sliced apples and covered in a mixture of beaten eggs, milk, and sugar that bakes up into a creamy dense custard wrapping each apple slice in a sweet and sugary cloud.

My heart feels love through food and my Memere showed love through her cooking, so not only was it the perfect meal to transition into the clear liquids restriction that would go into effect at midnight in preparation for surgery the next day, but it also filled up my soul on the eve of a day I did not want to face.

Have you ever worried so much about something happening that you couldn't even imagine how you would get through it, but then that fear becomes a reality and you are suddenly a warrior? Cool, calm, and absolutely in control? That's me. I worry about every possible scenario. I create horrifying scenes in my head and imagine the pain and fear so vividly that I can actually physically feel it, but when I actually go through the situation and my worst fear is no longer irrational but a reality, I become unstoppable and oddly want to fight the fear alone. I take on an "I've got this" attitude and walk into the woods with my bow on my back and a pocket full of arrows. Ready. Steady.

And this is exactly how I walked into the emergency room a few hours after my grand luncheon. Hands covered in blood and shaking uncontrollably…yet completely calm in my solitude.

"I am having a miscarriage," I said firmly and unemotionally.

I had rehearsed these words and watched this scene unfold for weeks in the movie in my head. The girl in the movie was sobbing and hunched over while being walked into the ER by a loving husband, who had wrapped a blanket and his arms around her, a look of deep sadness in his wounded eyes at the realization of the loss of his first child.

Yet I here I was, not shedding a tear, standing tall, intensely focused on the tiny circles in the registration wallpaper and all alone.

I had called Charlie from the bathroom when I felt the first warm gush of blood and again when I drove myself to the ER. I had tried his desk and his cell phone both times with no answer at either. I had called him a third time from the triage room when the nurse asked who brought me and I explained that I drove myself but that my husband would be arriving any minute. I was sure he would be. I had left a handwritten note on the table that said, "I tried to call you, come to the hospital."

But time ticked on.

As I lay on the table in stirrups in a sterile room waiting to be examined, the door finally opened and there stood Charlie. His eyes were bloodshot and I could immediately smell whiskey and cigarettes. I went from wishing he was there to wishing he wasn't. How foolish of me to think that the movie in my head was actually reality. This entire relationship had been a movie so far starring Charlie in the lead role.

"Where have you been?" I asked, tears of anger finally burning in the corners of my eyes.

I honestly can't remember what the answer was, and I didn't even care anymore. The doctor had come in to examine me and let me know that he called my doctor, who was in the OR prepping for surgery, and the ER staff would prep me.

I don't know if the doctor heard the sadness and fear in my voice when I explained that I had almost died of a postpartum hemorrhage only a few years prior and was afraid that I would hemorrhage again, or if he could smell the whiskey on Charlie's breath, but in that moment he became the sweetest, kindness human, let alone physician, I had ever met. He held my hand and reassured me that as long as he was with me absolutely nothing would happen to me. He pushed my bed all the way to the pre-op room and gave me a kiss on my forehead before parting ways with me and telling me that he would pray for me, a gesture that I will never, ever forget.

Sidenote about kindness. I was probably his thirtieth patient of the day. This was his job. Day in, day out. He could have treated me like just another number, but he took a few moments out of his day to make me feel comfortable and loved. Kindness can heal, and it is free and easy. Be kind. You never know what kind of battle someone is fighting.

Surgery didn't take long and I was heading home a few hours later with instructions to rest for a few days before returning to work.

I was fighting some significant depression. Charlie didn't seem too affected, and in retrospect I can sort of understand how he wasn't connected to this baby yet. I was the one feeling a physical change and seeing the physical signs and symptoms of pregnancy and miscarriage. It was unfair of me to expect the same emotional reaction from him; however, the support for *me* could have been stronger, so it was a welcome Monday when I went back to work.

Not long after the miscarriage, I found myself gravitating toward Ed again. He was, after all, my lifetime rock that I leaned on. I started to think about a conversation that I replayed in my head often.

Ed and I had shared a fairly intense and intimate conversation a few months before Charlie and I got married. He asked me if I was "sure". I remember feeling defensive and taken aback, almost offended, like he didn't trust my judgement. Now I know that I was instantly defensive because the answer was no, I wasn't sure.

He told me that he was happy for me but he needed to tell me that he always thought he would be the man waiting for me at the end of the aisle. Whoa, what? When? Where and how?

I was a little ticked. How could he tell me this right before I was going to get married? How could he tell me this now? But if I am being completely honest and open, I felt happy, too. How sweet that someone could love me so much that he actually pictured himself marrying me…but that was silly because duh, we were best friends, and duh times two, we lived really far away from each other. And oh yeah, I had a son and he had a career that he was building. I would just be in the way of that. And that is honestly how I reacted. It wasn't until years later that I realized what he was trying to tell me. By the time I understood, it was much too late.

A month or so later Ed called, and to my surprise he

was in town to see me. He was on his way to Wisconsin for something work related and sidetracked his trip to surprise me. It was a Friday night, and earlier that day Charlie had a medical test that knocked him out for the day and night. My girlfriend, April, had asked me to meet her and a group of her work friends at a Thai restaurant/martini bar for appetizers and drinks. Since Charlie was super out of it, he told me to go and have a good time with my friends.

Halfway through my second cosmopolitan, my phone buzzed and lit up, displaying Ed's name. I was so excited, as I was every time his name came up on my phone, that I nearly threw my phone trying to answer. "Hey"! I said excitedly. "Can you hear me okay?" I shouted as I simultaneously moved from the restaurant to the front door where I could hear better, all while giving April the "one second" sign with my index finger.

"Just calling to say hi and see how you are. What are y'all up to?" he asked.

I told him that we were out for drinks and Thai food, and when he asked me where, I started to get a tiny bit suspicious.

"On Liberty Street in Morris," I said slowly, almost in a question instead of a statement while looking up and down the road to see if maybe, just maybe…but again, this is real life and my mind was probably just… And then like a magic trick that deceives the eyes, *poof*, there he was. Standing on the sidewalk, right in front of my eyes stood my best friend. I stood, staring at him for a few seconds in disbelief before I realized that I was still holding the phone to my ear. With a martini-induced squeal and some sort of cheerleader-style bunny rabbit jump, I threw my arms around his neck and squeezed him until we almost fell backwards.

This is how we began the last night that we would share together as best friends before becoming complete strangers. It's funny, looking back, I should have known. This night was perfect. Too perfect, actually. We shared a hilarious meal—me, Thai noodles and spring rolls, Ed, my Southern bestie, ordering a steak in a Thai restaurant and being served one of the biggest T-bones that either of us had ever seen. So big, in fact, that we thought they must have had to send someone to the store to buy one before preparing it. Hours of riding around in his warm pristine truck, visiting old stomping grounds like the high school football field, first job sites, and the house where he lived during high school. Singing to Steve Earle at the top of our lungs as we rode along the river and watched the steam rise from the cold winter air hitting the still warm autumn water. And finally seeing the sun coming up while we filled our bellies with sweet sticky cinnamon rolls from the same truck stop restaurant that used to serve as a late night postprom hangout when we were kids. I write country songs, and I don't think I could write a better one than this picture. Until my phone rang and everything changed.

Charlie. Shit.

I was so wrapped up in this perfect, innocent night that I had forgotten about Charlie. It was the most fun that I had experienced in years. The freest, the most relaxed I had been in so long that for a few hours, I had completely forgotten about my life.

"Where are you?" a half-asleep Charlie asked, somewhat concerned but mostly perplexed. I explained where I was and where I had been, and he told me to have fun. But the fun was over.

I will never forget the disappointed look on Ed's face.

"You didn't tell your husband where you were?"

Like a child who was in trouble, I tried to back up my story and explain that he had a procedure and was sound asleep and that he didn't care where I was anyway. But the more I explained, the worse I sounded, and the worse I sounded, the more I explained until I just gave up defeated and went home. I wanted to scream that he was right, that he had been right. I didn't have good judgement. I *wasn't* sure, and now I was miserable and stuck, and Charlie probably drank after his anesthesia and that was why it was 5 a.m. before he finally started looking for me. I wanted to scream that I was drowning in regret and shame and that tonight was the first time that I had felt like myself in years and that for once in my life, I was happy and free again, even if it was just for a few hours…but I didn't. I hung my head and went home. I took the fall. I looked like the bad wife. I looked irresponsible and disrespectful and immature. So I did what any guilty wife would do—I apologized to Ed and asked him to please let me make it right and invited him to my home to meet Charlie later that day.

This is where things went downhill even faster. I have a certain standard of how I like to keep my things and portray my lifestyle. I take pride in how I live my life and want to be perceived only in that light. But things were rough at home. Charlie's drinking, style, and personality had taken over our home quite a bit, and I, like clay, molded to his ways. We smoked cigarettes inside and hung Beatles posters on our walls where my Hobby Lobby decor had once hung.

The whole house smelled of patchouli, Charlie's choice of cologne, instead of apple candles, and it made the place smell like a head shop. Things were clean but heavy, both energetically and physically. It was not a time that I was proud of.

A few short hours after sunrise, Ed walked in my front door. Charlie, still in his sweats, barely stood to shake Ed's hand. Not out of disrespect, but in the hope of getting attention for his procedure the day before. Charlie thrived on getting attention. Ed, however, was so uncomfortable in our home that he barely noticed. I can't say I blame him because as uncomfortable as he was, I was squirming in my shoes, praying that I would just disappear in the blink of an eye like the main character on *I Dream of Jeannie*. Blink, blink…nope. Still here.

We decided to go out to breakfast before Ed had to take off and continue on to Wisconsin. He had goals and life plans, after all. We went to a local family restaurant in town and ordered our breakfast. Charlie asked Ed a few questions about his sport, and although he was answering them, an awkward silence screamed its ugly shriek. Too quiet for an onlooker to notice, but so ear-piercingly loud it was hard for Ed or me to ignore. Charlie just didn't even see or feel it. He was hungry from not eating the day before and didn't seem to notice the intense sadness written all over my face. I was disappointed in myself. This was not the life I wanted Ed to see me in; it was one of my lowest points, hiding behind lies and betrayal.

When breakfast was over and we said our awkward goodbyes and went our separate ways, the excitement that had been running through my veins not even twelve hours prior had run cold. Ed drove to the north in his big, beautiful truck, and Charlie and I drove to the south in his beat-up car. A moment that is still so real to me I can feel the sadness welling up in my chest as I type. The image that Ed had of me was destroyed. The girl he thought I was was gone, the image in his head, tainted. I wanted to scream at Charlie to stop the car, but I sat silently, tears flowing down my cheeks, and I turned to look out the passenger window as we drove farther and farther away. I would soon find out how far away that car would actually take me.

In true "me" fashion, I dove right back into The Next American Superstar competition and hit the ground running. When I'm ready to move on from something, I tend to arrive at my next challenge with a hunger that is unstoppable. Sometimes I'm so obsessed with greeting my new challenge that I unapologetically close myself into a room and emerge only when I am finished or exhausted. It's a practice that would follow me well into my songwriting years.

A few weeks later I was on a flight to Dallas by myself. The Next American Superstar team had two full days planned that would end with a concert at Gilley's in Dallas. Gilley's is a big deal. It's a large honky tonk where two-stepping Texans arrive ready to dance the night away, complete with a mechanical bull that made its way to fame via the John Travolta movie, *Urban Cowboy*. Two days of public appearances, signing sessions, XM radio interviews, rehearsals, sound checks, fast-paced lunches on the move, and drawn-out fancy dinners on the top floor of the tallest building in Dallas were on the agenda. Shiny town cars picked up all six of us girls from our hotel, where we waited on marble entryways alongside rich businessmen, and not just any rich men—*Texas* rich men in ten-gallon hats, bolo ties, and snakeskin boots that peeked out of their cuffed suit pants. With big toothy grins holding fat cigars, they smiled, and with a tip of their head they slowly drawled out a "ma'am" as we walked to our waiting car.

Speaking of cars, the only car that didn't pick me up was the car that was supposed to pick me up from the airport when I landed, leaving me stranded in a state where I knew no one except for one person. Ed.

I called Ed no less than ten times in a row, praying that he would tell me that he was coming right through town and could pick me up and that maybe we could have dinner and why yes, he would love to come to my show in Dallas. But since this is real life, no such miracle occurred. No luck. No answer. Finally, as the lights were going off and the airport was closing, a town car pulled in right as my phone died. Ed never did call back on that trip, and the next time I saw him, it was a year or so later and he was on TV. On a rainy Sunday morning I watched him win a tournament. I was so damn proud of him that I called and left him a voicemail telling him how proud of him I was and that I knew he was busy but maybe he could call me back sometime and catch me up on all of the great things that were happening for him. I told him that I loved him bunches (kind of our thing for years) and to call me when he could. I wanted him to know about my career too. I was still trying to get back my worth with him, and it is still something that I struggle with to this day.

He called me back a few days after that message and told me that I shouldn't be telling him that I loved him. I was married and he was in a serious relationship and that just wasn't right to say anymore. I was humiliated and hurt. I had never meant anything disrespectful by telling him that, and it was apparent that he still looked down on me.

That was the last time I talked to Ed as friends. We would have one more encounter in person and two more phone conversations before cutting our ties completely, something I have never been able to heal from. I have, however, learned many lessons and have written many songs pulled from this pain. One lesson is this—don't be afraid to tell those you love that you love them. Yes, it cost me a friendship, but I stayed true to myself. I am a pourer of love, a complete giver of my heart. Many times since this painful experience, I have nearly stopped myself from showing love, but then I remember that's not my gig. And because I have kept myself open to showing love and being loved, I have experienced what it feels like to be fully enveloped by unconditional love instead of love with conditions.

Dallas was a turning point in my career. Standing on a famous stage in front of a packed room full of people who know the words to your songs is like nothing I can explain. The backing band was a group of players from L.A. and Nashville. There were two audio/visual techs running cameras and a killer light show. This was a *real* show. Before the other girls and I were whisked off in a Cadillac SUV from dinner to the show, we had some time to get to know each other, and they were inspiring and intriguing. Almost all of the girls lived in Nashville with the exception of one who was from California. A few of the girls had good starts to their careers and I was envious, in a healthy way, of their professional wins. I wanted that for myself. They were living my dream and for a few days, I got to live it too. Only when the two days were up, they were flying back to Nashville to continue on in Music City, and I was flying back to Chicago to face what I had left behind. A sad, sad heart and a husband who was drinking away our marriage.

Have you ever felt like you were on top of the world one minute and then in the next, you lost everything? That's how I felt when I returned home. Dallas was such an eye-opening experience, and it made me see in bold color all of the dreams that I was holding on to. I wanted to take on the world. I was ready. Maybe we could move to Nashville. Maybe I could just move to Nashville. I could take Daniel and go…I had planned that once, you know. Back in the days of the duplex. I spent a month researching and lining up job interviews and daycare interviews. I had found an apartment that I could afford and had carefully planned my move to Brentwood, Tennessee. I hadn't told anyone my plans, but they were solid and moving forward. But as the time drew closer and closer and reality set it, I got scared and changed my mind. Little did I know that as I canceled my plans to go to Nashville, someone who would soon change my life forever had just moved back from Nashville, broken by Music City's relentless grip, and he and I were about to collide in ways that no one could have ever seen coming.

Chapter 6
Bar Room Walls

Andrea and Johnny and Charlie and I had become friends who were more like family. We had inside jokes and went to each other's children's birthday parties. We spent holidays and lazy summer weekend nights together. We were neighbors who lived across the street from each other and had watched a handful of families come and go in the quiet cul-de-sac where we resided.

One of our favorite things to do was "garage sit", a term we coined after a few months of chilling in one of our garages and talking all night long while sipping a few Twisted Teas. This would become a weekly event, usually starting on a Friday night and ending on a Sunday with Sunday night football and chili, and a few bonfires thrown in for good measure. Andrea's youngest daughter and Daniel were only a year apart and would play together until one of them dozed off on the couch while watching movies. We were practically inseparable. Andrea used to ask me to go see a band with her that her coworker, Terry, sang in, but we ended up couch sitting so much that we didn't actually make it out until over a year later.

Andrea was one of the first to recognize that Charlie had a problem. We would share concerned glances from across the table or room when the nights went from fun to "maybe time to call it a night". Still, I continued on because, you know, disappointment, pride, and fear.

In the summer of 2006, after a weekend of garage sitting, I went to the doctor for some ongoing stomach pain I had been experiencing. Twenty-five minutes later I was holding an ultrasound picture of a tiny bubble. I was six weeks pregnant. But just like the summer before, there was a problem. My numbers were once again not climbing and no heartbeat had been detected yet. I was also having some light cramping and spotting. My doctor sent me home to wait and watch. I could not believe that I was going to walk this path again. Charlie and I had been very distant, and truthfully the only time this could have happened was once after a vulnerable moment of feeling like I needed to do everything to save our marriage. But six weeks was a long time ago, and things had already gone even further downhill by then.

Sometimes I think we try to look for signs as to whether we are supposed to stay in a situation or leave that situation. For instance, I currently know that we should start looking for another home. We moved into our current home when our kids were all still around, and it has served us well. However, we are now at a point where we could easily downsize. I am emotionally attached to this house for many reasons, and even though I know deep down it would serve us better to leave, I still look for reasons to stay. Why would I do that? If I have the knowledge that moving would benefit us financially and physically, then why would I try to look for signs that we're supposed to stay? Two reasons: comfort and fear. It's easy to stay comfortable, even if a situation doesn't make complete sense, because fear of *not* being comfortable kicks in. So we try to make a rational decision with emotionally driven thoughts.

So when I found out that I was pregnant, I thought *this* was the sign I needed. That *this* was going to fix my marriage. That *this* would change everything. So when the baby's tiny heartbeat was finally detected, everything just seemed to fall into place. We went through all of the motions and did everything we were supposed to do as expectant parents.

The first twelve weeks were a roller-coaster. I was placed on bed rest due to some cramping and spotting, but our weekly ultrasounds and bloodwork showed a thriving fetus. Every minute of the day I worried that I was about to miscarry again, and I suffered from severe morning sickness that lasted all day, so most days were filled with the same routine. Wake up and get sick. Charlie would make me a Carnation Instant Breakfast on ice every day before he left for work, and that seemed to get me through to lunchtime. I was allowed to recline in a recliner, so I would walk to the living room (I was allowed to walk from one room to the other as long as I wasn't up for more than five minutes) and set up camp in our overstuffed recliner. Around lunchtime my mom or Memere or Pepere would deliver lunch for me. At 1 p.m. TLC would play back-to-back episodes of *A Baby*

Story. At 2 p.m. Rachel Ray cooked up dishes with EVOO on the Food Network, and at 3 p.m. *The Ellen Show* would round out my day before Daniel got off the bus, and a few hours later Charlie came home. Twelve weeks of the same exact routine. Once a week my mom would pick me up and take me to the doctor for a check-up. At exactly twelve weeks along, my doctor released me for light activity, and twelve hours later my sweet Grandma Fish died.

Grandma had been moved to a nursing home in the burbs and the yellow house on Main Street had been sold. Every time I would drive by that house, a physical pain would zing right through the center of my belly.

Moments become memories in the blink of an eye. Pay attention and absorb it all. You will miss the smell of the kitchen, the way the floor feels under your feet, and what it feels like to swing open a door and see your loved one's face, and you'll be glad you paid attention while you could.

The day before she died, I had walked out to my back patio with a bag of birdseed and sat in the morning sun, an activity that entertained me way more than it should have, but hey, it had been a long twelve weeks. I watched the birds peck at the ground in search of food. I took a handful of seeds out and tossed it around. The birds pecked a little and then turned their heads with no interest. Huh. That was odd. Birds love to eat. So I tried again. I scooped up the seeds and tossed them out a little deeper into the yard. Nothing. And then all of the birds flew away.

I could feel it coming long before I could see it. Giant, hot tears blurred my vision and stung my eyes. My cheeks were hot and red and now wet with salty tears dripping down my neck.

If I couldn't get a bird to eat, how was I going to get a baby to eat, and if I couldn't get a baby to eat, how was I going to be able to keep it alive? Even though it doesn't seem logical, those were my thoughts at the time. In those few moments of breakdown, I was sure that anyone who couldn't feed a bird was unfit to be a decent mother and that I had already failed. I lost the baby last year and this one was doing its best to skip town too. My body, invaded by endometriosis at such a young age, was not capable of a normal pregnancy without trying to kill me during and after. Hearing other women's stories of easy pregnancies and bodies that were born for breeding just made me feel worse. Less than. Incapable.

Maybe I should have stopped watching back-to-back episodes of *A Baby Story*. Ugh.

The house phone rang at 4:30 a.m. the very next morning (yes, we had cell phones back then, but the house phone eradication had not yet swept the nation). It was my mom. She was speaking to me like I was six years old again.

"Honey, your dad didn't want me to call you because he's afraid you'll get in the car and drive and you can't yet, but Grandma fell. She had a stroke."

"Is she okay?" I managed to squeak out.

"No, honey, she's not. She's gone."

Just a short twelve hours prior, Grandma Fish had called me to see how my doctor appointment went. She knew I was at my twelve-week mark and that we would find out if things were actually going to progress into a healthy pregnancy at my appointment that day.

I will never forget her words.

She said, "How is the baby?"

To which I replied, "They said everything is real good, Gram. They said I can do light activity and the baby is very healthy."

To which she then replied, "Oh good. That's what I've been waiting to hear."

So when she passed twelve hours later, the first thing that went through my mind was, *Oh my God, she waited to die until she knew that the baby was okay.*

And just like that, she was gone. We buried her on September fifth, and a few months later on March sixth, we welcomed our screaming 8 pound, 1 ounce baby girl into the world.

Marleyna was born via a fairly uneventful normal delivery with Heather by my side. Charlie was there too, but Heather's presence kept me rock steady through the six-hour induced labor and delivery. This delivery was a much calmer experience than delivering my son. Everything was planned out the week prior.

I arrived at 6 a.m. to get cozy in my sunny, warm, private room with wood floors and beautiful artwork hiding the cabinets that housed the medical equipment needed in the event of an emergency. The hospital's labor and delivery unit buzzed with excited family members and fresh, rested staff who doted on the patients as if they were royalty. At 7 a.m. my bright and cheery doctor appeared in the doorway with a steaming cup of coffee and orders to start a Pitocin drip. By 10 a.m. things were progressing nicely. There were big labor balls ready to rock back and forth on and warm socks and blankets to keep the shivering delivering mothers warm. Everything about this experience was night and day from my first. My mom, aunt, and Memere camped out in the family waiting area, and once in a while my mom would pop her head in, which went like this.

Me: "I want my mom. Can someone go get my mom?"

A few minutes later, my excited mom would stand by my bed caressing my head.

Me: "I need my mom to go... Mom, can you go?"

A little wounded but understanding, she would slink out and return to camp, then...

Me: "I need my mom, can someone get my mom?"

This song and dance happened half a dozen times until it was finally time to get the epidural. Oh, sweet heaven. Considering my first delivery where there was no time for an epidural, this was my first experience. I wanted to kiss the anesthesiologist who placed the needle in my back while I leaned into Heather's torso. She held my rounded back steady while he placed and taped the tubing. Kudos to Heather. It paid to have a friend who was an L&D nurse.

A few hours and pushes later, the doctor announced that we had a healthy baby girl. She was pink and chubby and screaming with perfect rosebud lips that were so round, we could see them on the ultrasound pictures months before her arrival.

And this is the story of sweet Marleyna coming into this world. Charlie was a good support but left shortly after her delivery to go home and make announcements and take a shower. He never did come back that night, and when I finally talked to him he was already a few drinks in, so I hung with my new baby girl and some of my nursing friends, who were just coming in on the afternoon shift. Not even the birth of his daughter could snap him out of Glenlivet's grip. As I sat cross-legged on the hospital bed unwrapping this tiny, warm newborn, I knew that life was changing fast, and in more ways than one.

After bringing Marley home, I decided that I was going to stay home with her for a while. Daycare was expensive, and for two kids it would have cost me more than I made. So after years of working full time, I suddenly found myself a stay-at-home mom. I feel like I was very blessed to have had this time. Not only was I learning to take care of an infant all over again, but I was learning to take care of myself too. Charlie's drinking was at its all-time worst. He was late coming home from work nearly every day. He fell a few times, once breaking our coffee table and once injuring his eye so badly that he required stitches to close the bleeding gap. His speech was slurred, but not so much that it was totally evident—in a way, that made me question if it was actually alcohol or if something else was going on.

One night, after meeting Charlie at the front door and hearing that slur in his voice, I asked him, like I did every night, if he had been drinking. His answer was always the same: "no", with a slight hint of disgust that I was asking *again*. This time I told him that he either needed to tell me the truth or I was going to take him to the hospital to see if he was having a stroke. It was *that* evident. He swore up and down that he hadn't been drinking. He insinuated that I must have been tired or not feeling well because clearly it was me and not him. He hadn't changed at all, but I had changed a lot, and he was worried about me.

For a moment, I bought it. I had, after all, just had a baby and a lifestyle change. Maybe it was postpartum hormones, maybe I was paranoid or hallucinating from lack of sleep, but on this particular night, long after Charlie fell asleep in a deep coma-like snooze, covered in sweat, I walked out to his truck and searched it.

The feeling I had when I pulled that first empty bottle of whiskey out from under his driver's side seat is indescribable, really, but I'll try.

My face was burning red and I could feel my heart pounding in my chest and my neck. How *dare* he make me feel like I was crazy. I stood in the dark driveway holding the empty bottle and staring into space as if a spirit was going to come down and explain to me what had just happened. Instead, I walked quickly and purposefully into the bedroom, flipped on the overhead light, and cleared my throat. Nothing.

Eh hem… I tried again a little louder. This time Charlie squinted, distorted his face and tried to shield the light from his eyes. "What in the hell are you doing?" he asked.

"What in the hell is *this*?" I asked back.

"Jonelle, I don't know what that is or where you found it," he said, annoyed and already arranging his pillows to get back to sleep.

"In your *truck*," I said, now speaking in short sentences.

And that was it. Before I could get any sort of explanation, he was back to sleep.

The next morning as he was getting ready to leave for work and I was rocking the baby, he looked at me with a quizzical look of concern.

"Are you okay?" he asked worriedly. He went on, "You were sleepwalking last night. You must have been dreaming because you were yelling at me about some bottle you thought you found in my truck, but you had been sound asleep right before. I should have taken a video…you were blaming me for having an empty bottle of booze in my truck. I had to lay you back down so that you would calm down and go back to sleep." He went on further still. "I think you should talk to someone. You have me worried."

And with that, he went off to work, leaving me standing in the kitchen, burp cloth over my shoulder and last night's makeup still caked on my tired eyes.

But suddenly I didn't feel tired. Numb—that's what I felt next. Numb.

I know that I had really walked out and searched his truck. That happened…right? Gosh, I was really tired and…no wait, this really happened, right? I didn't say much more to Charlie that week, but I did ask Andrea to confirm my next finding, if there was one.

This cycle of Charlie coming home from work slurring and denying my accusations and then finding empty bottles continued on and on. Most days he was extremely functional, going to work and attending school functions. He was even coherent enough to stay with the kids while I ran out to get groceries or on the rare occasion that I got to have dinner with a friend, but something had changed with him. I just couldn't put my finger on it.

Sometimes on a weekend, a music buddy would come over and they would really do it up. These were my least favorite weekends. I would reminisce about the past and dream about the days that my Friday and Saturday nights were filled with stage lights and loud guitars. I loved being home with my babies, but being home with my babies while a basement full of intoxicated, non-working musicians bitched about the music scene was not my idea of a good time.

Sometimes on a Sunday evening after the party weekend was over, I would beg Charlie to come clean with me. With himself. Many times, literally on my knees while he sat in the overstuffed chair from my duplex that was now ripped up from the cat, I would kneel in front of him and take his shaky hands, pleading with him to go to an AA meeting. Talk to someone. Anyone.

But Charlie knew it all. He didn't need help. He would stop if it made me feel better because he could, at any time…but it wasn't necessary to go to a meeting. Those were for alcoholics, and he wasn't an alcoholic. So Sunday through Tuesday would be good. My clear-eyed and non-slurring husband would arrive home from work on time and we would eat dinner and play with the kids before putting them to bed. And then came Wednesday, and it would start all over again.

Andrea knew that things were really going downhill after I put her on bottle watch. She had asked me once when I sat in her house just staring off into space if it was bad enough that I thought I should leave. To be honest, this wasn't the first time I had thought about this question. I had told myself after every chair intervention that if things didn't change this time, I would have no choice. But Monday would come and things would go back to normal and I would just walk the path. Go through the motions, once again.

When the baby was three months old, on a random Saturday, I caught the flu. I felt it coming on hard, and within a few hours after the first chill, I was down for the count with a high fever and flat on my back in bed. It was only 5 p.m. and dinner still had to be made, baths given, the house locked up, and lights turned off before I could think about going to sleep. I was always the last to go to bed because Charlie usually fell asleep in the chair, and I lived in fear of the house being left wide open while we were sleeping, so I would put everyone to bed and close up the house myself.

But on this particular Saturday night, there was no way I could do it. I was way too sick, so Charlie told me to go to bed, he had it taken care of. Plus, Daniel was nearly nine years old and could help. I couldn't even argue, I lugged my tired and feverish body to the bedroom, where I landed on the bed and stayed in one position until I heard the baby scream so loud that I sat straight up out of a sound sleep. Breathing hard, I sat in the darkness, disoriented about what day or time it was, trying to determine if I was just dreaming or if I actually heard the baby screaming…and then I heard it again.

I threw back the covers and bolted into the living room, where all of the lights were still blazing, the TV was blaring, and the front door and windows had been left wide open. The sound of infant screams was coming from somewhere nearby…12:35 a.m. It was 12:35 a.m. My eyes were starting to focus now.

Daniel was sound asleep in his jeans on the couch, and Charlie was sitting up in the recliner holding his empty arms out, looking dazed and confused. His eyes, bloodshot red.

"Where is she?!" I screamed, looking around frantically.

Charlie gave me a blank look, like he could hear me but didn't understand the words I was saying.

One more loud cry and I saw her. Barely wrapped in

her pink blanket between the recliner and the end table was Marleyna.

He had dropped her and didn't even know it.

I scooped her up and he stood, trying to steady himself to see her through the tears in his eyes. But it was too late. I pulled her away and shouted "No!" and told him to get away from us.

I had no idea if she was hurt, but she was cold from the night air blowing in, so I put her in her car seat, and with a warm blanket wrapped around her, I drove to the Emergency Room. I wasn't sure what I was going to say, I just felt like I needed someone qualified to tell me that she was okay. The guilt that I had for going to sleep early that night was overwhelming, and I needed another capable adult to look at her and tell me that everything was going to be alright.

She was totally and completely fine that night. I had told the attending physician that my husband had fallen asleep and she wiggled out of his arms, but he was the same guy who had given Charlie his eye stitches a few weeks prior. He was, however, kind enough to smile and lie to me, saying that he, too, once had that happen with his own baby and that I shouldn't beat myself up too badly. "Kids are resilient," he said.

Charlie didn't drink for a while after that night. I think it scared him enough to straighten up a bit, but for me, it was much too late. I didn't say a word to him about leaving but got my stuff in order in case it came to that. We had fallen out of love and things were just tense and unwelcoming at our house. Even without the booze.

I decided that I better start looking for a job again. If

I was going to find myself in the position of being a single mother for the second time in my life, then I needed to be prepared. But my search left me empty-handed. I needed something that enabled me to pay for daycare or something at night so that my parents or Charlie, should I dare to trust him again, could help me out with the kids.

I was a mess and I hardly did anything for myself anymore, including makeup, hair, or the big one—music. I was barely eating and I was losing weight. Andrea was really starting to see this take a toll on me. She was, after all, one of my closest friends, and living just across the street allowed her to see me day in and day out. I spent the summer in limbo and there was no hiding from that.

Do you guys remember Nextel phones? They were huge at that time. You could walkie-talkie another Nextel user and the phone would chirp like a bird. They were great.

Anyway, it was a Saturday night in October and I was at home cleaning out a closet. My parents had offered to take the kids home for the night so that I could get some stuff done. It had been a quiet day with no kids, and I plugged away at making as much progress as I could on the closet.

Chirrrrrp!

"Heyyyyy, J!" Andrea's voice came blaring through my Nextel, plugged in on my nightstand.

I sighed and kept folding piles of jeans that were now too big for me. Stress does funny things to a body.

Chirrrrrp!

"JJJJJJJJJJAYYYYY, pick up! Come and have a beer with me!"

Sigh again. She knew I was home. I couldn't keep ignoring her. So I chirped her back and she begged me to come and have *one* beer at Clayton's Tap with her. Clayton's is a family-owned bar and grill in the historic downtown district that regularly has local bands and fun crowds, and her friend from work was playing that night.

I was wearing a baseball hat and not a stitch of makeup. Well, maybe a little of yesterday's eye makeup, but you get the picture.

I told her no. Emphatically, no. I was in no mood to be in a bar and I hadn't showered in two days. I had dried formula on my shirt and under it, no bra. I was content folding jeans and sorting summer clothes from winter in anticipation of the changing seasons.

Chirrrrrp!

Now it was Johnny. He knew I didn't have the kids, and in big brother fashion, he promised me that he would come and drag me out of the house because I needed to get out of the damn house and actually live a little.

So with aggravation and the motivator of shutting them up, I put on a bra, changed my shirt, brushed my teeth, and grabbed my keys. I considered putting fresh makeup on but settled on keeping my hat down low to cover most of my eyes. I was going for *one* beer anyway and then back home to work on my closet project.

As I pulled into the parking lot and saw all of the cars and activity around the bar, I started to clam up. I should have put some makeup on or at least done my hair. The land of the living looked a whole lot prettier than I did, and now I felt like I wanted to go back home and hide again. I was safe among my jeans, they didn't judge.

So I chirped Andrea from the parking lot and told her I wasn't coming in.

She begged. She gave me a guilt trip. She begged again.

Finally, I gave in, under one circumstance. I would come in if she didn't tell her friend that I was a singer. I didn't want to discuss it. I didn't want to be asked to go up and sing. I just wanted to blend in with the crowd, have my one beer, and go home.

It had been a long time since I had been surrounded by barroom walls. Understand this—bars are my office. They are where I go to work. When I work, I don't drink until my job is done. Afterwards I might have a beer or a glass of wine, but if I have a four-hour show, I can't drink and sing. It's not pretty. Just trust me. So when I talk about loving the bar feel, don't confuse that with me loving to drink alcohol. It's just the feeling, the energy, the vibe that makes it home to me, so when I walked into the bar, my heart skipped a beat.

If being numb was a one on a scale of one to ten, then I was now at a two. I felt a little something, but still not much.

I ordered a Corona Light with lime and pushed my way to the back room, where I could see the lights and hear the smack of the drums. I found Andrea and John at a table near the back, and she squealed with giddiness when she saw me. A banner across the back of the stage with the band name sprawled across in neon letters read "The Clients".

Holy shit.

Like, The Clients that my ex paid for me to sing with years before? Yep. Those Clients.

They were playing their last song of the set when I joined Andrea and John, and then they made their "we'll be right back" break announcement just as I was sitting down.

Andrea, all but bouncing up and down, was calling to her work friend, Terry, to come and meet me. Terry was the guitar player and was just unstrapping his blue Fender Strat from across his chest. He stepped off the stage, wiped his forehead with a blue Coors Light towel, stuck his hand out, smiled, and shook the hand of his future wife.

Chapter 7
Tequila & Whiskey

NEITHER OF US COULD HAVE known what God had planned. This is why you trust the journey. We are a living example. I could go on and on about what would have happened had I not gone to Clayton's that night, but you won't truly hear me until you open your mind and your heart and let go of trying to have control of your future. Trusting the journey isn't about living every day carefree with no responsibility for your actions, but rather trusting that when moments blindside us, like the Clayton's night, we trust that there is something bigger than us with a plan that we couldn't even begin to dream up. If you take anything away from this book—anything at all—please let it be this: when things are feeling hopeless and dark, your hero could very possibly be waiting around the corner. Do not ever give up.

"Hi there, I'm Terry," he said with warm hands and denim-blue eyes. He was about the same height as me and had wisps of dark hair peeking out from underneath a beat-up backwards ball cap. He looked like a musician and not just because he had a guitar strapped on just a few minutes prior, he just had that musician look. I've been around a few and they have a look. He smiled a closed-mouth smile, and charming dimples appeared on each of his cheeks. He gave Andrea a genuine hug and I instantly liked his easy-to-be-with disposition. He seemed relaxed and a sense of calm just sort of waved over me.

"This is my friend Jonelle," said Andrea excitedly, "and she sings."

Sense of calm gone.

What in the actual hell. I told her not to tell him. I specifically told her not to…

"Want to come up and sing one?" The silent argument in my head was interrupted by Terry's voice.

"Noooo…I'm good. Thank you, though. I came to watch you guys pla—"

"Come on, are you chicken?" he asked in a joking tone that was sweet yet sassy all at the same time.

My head tilted to the left and I gave him a confident and somewhat smirky half-smile.

"What songs do you know that I know?" No one was going to call me a chicken.

We settled on a Linda Ronstadt song, "When Will I Be Loved", and after their break was over and they were a few songs in, Terry called me up to sing. In my hat… wearing yesterday's mascara. *Thank God I at least changed my formula-stained shirt*, I thought as I walked up the stage stairs. I shook all of the rest of the band members' hands, a gesture that is professional and shows respect when you are taking another band's stage. I cleared my throat and adjusted my mic. The crowd was waiting with anticipation and I had no idea what was about to go down. I just knew that I had been on my floor shoving donation pants into a Hefty bag an hour ago, and now I was under hot stage lights with a crowd of people cheering me on.

Terry pointed his guitar toward me and with serious eye contact, counted me in.

"I've been cheated, been mistreated," I sang. "When will I be loved?"

Whoa. Holy. What? The harmony was coming from where…the actual heavens above? Nope. It was Terry. We locked in on a harmony six words into the first song we sang together, and he looked as surprised as I did as the crowd danced and cheered. We both relaxed and had a fun three-and-a-half minutes on stage together. When the song ended, the crowd was chanting, "One more song! One more song!" I honestly can't remember if we did one more or not because all I can remember is the line "when will I be loved" and the harmony that changed my life, literally forever.

I stayed for a little while longer before heading home. I got one more chance to talk to Terry before he played the last set of the night. He asked me if I would be into doing a duo thing. He had been looking for someone to partner up with, and it was obvious that our voices were good together, so before leaving I jotted my number down on a torn piece of paper and dropped it onto his pedal board before walking out. Numbness on a scale of one to ten…now eleven. I could feel again.

I wish I could tell you that this is our love story. That

it was happily ever after from this day forward. That my prince swept me off my feet and we lived in a little house with a white picket fence forever and ever, amen. But we would have to endure many painful, trying, emotional, and heart-wrenching days and nights before our actual love story began. We would first become bandmates, then best friends, and eventually navigate our way through two difficult and ugly divorces before finally having our chance and space to grow into a deep and meaningful partnership. This story is about the day I met him. This was also the day I re-met myself, but it would be a long, long time before the two of us were joined together as one.

A few weeks went by and the highly anticipated phone call that I was waiting for had not come. When Terry mentioned doing a "duo thing", a tiny flame flickered inside of me. This could give me the chance to not only get back into music but to have a job that would allow me to be home with my kids during the day. Just like I had hoped for. But as the days ticked on, I lost hope a little at a time.

I finally broke down and asked Andrea if he had said anything at work, and she said that he had sounded excited about the idea of doing something with me and that I should try to call *him*. She gave me his number and I waited for a weekday to call. I wanted this to go the right way. I wanted to represent myself as professional and not too excited but show that my interest was piqued. So I dialed his number and to my surprise he answered on the first ring. In a hushed and faint whisper, he said "Hello?"

"Uh, hi. Uh, Terry, this is Jonelle, the singer from a few weeks ago. Um…I'm sorry, is this a bad time?"

He was literally whispering when he replied that he

was with his mom and that they had just called in hospice because she was going to die at any moment. He had answered my call because it was an 815 area code and that was the same as the hospice area code.

This was not going well.

I apologized profusely, and he reassured me that he would call me when things settled down. A few more weeks went by and he made good on his promise and called. He asked me if I could meet for lunch so we could discuss a few things. We agreed to meet at 4 p.m. on a Wednesday at a restaurant not far from my house.

I secured my mom to babysit and pulled on some old jeans and a graphic T. My hair was long and naturally wavy and it had been a year or more since I had colored it, so it was in its natural state—very boring brown. Still, I felt like I looked decent with light makeup and freshly shampooed hair, plus I didn't have any baby poop or spit up on me, so this was a win in my book.

I kissed my babies and drove to the restaurant and looked around nervously, but I didn't see Terry anywhere. I have a habit of being early so I took a seat in the lobby area and waited patiently. After about forty-five minutes I was starting to get concerned. Did I have the wrong day? Did he change his mind? Was I at the wrong place?

I didn't want to call and bother him again if he was driving, but after about an hour I decided to call. He didn't answer, but a few seconds later he called me back. I asked him if I was confused on the date and time for meeting up, and he nearly shouted into the phone, "I am *so* sorry. Oh my God, I'm getting out of the shower now and I'll be there in five minutes"…except that he lived forty-five minutes away. This was the first of many experiences that have been ruled by what we like to call "Terry Time".

Forty-five minutes later a very hurried and winded Terry came charging through the double doors, apologizing before he was even in all the way. I giggled at the way he was flustered and imagined him driving like a maniac all the way to the restaurant. Something about it was very funny to me, but I think it was because I was so relieved that he hadn't changed his mind.

I look back at that meeting and ponder something... There were two people seated behind us at a tall bar top table and they were having a heated conversation about child support and spousal support. As Terry and I started chatting while looking over the menu, the couple gradually began raising their voices. They were passionate about this subject, and it was clear that neither of them felt that the other was being fair. We exchanged curious glances over the table with each other as they grew louder and louder. Finally, it became so uncomfortable that we asked to be moved to a different table.

I clearly remember judging them. Is that the best thing to admit? No, but it's the most honest thing to admit. I remember thinking that they were a mess and that I felt sorry for them but was more annoyed with their back and forth arguing. I remember thinking, *My God, have some class, people.*

So here I was with my own personal life falling apart and I had the guts to judge someone else. Shame on me for thinking that I was any better than they were. Shame on me for feeling above someone and looking down on two complete strangers who were clearly in deep turmoil and emotional pain. I should have prayed for them. I should have sent a drink to their table incognito just to show them that there was still enough love in the world to get by. But I didn't. I judged, and years later, I figured out why.

They were living out my fears. They were facing the problems I didn't want to face by finally calling my marriage quits. They made *me* uncomfortable because I was about to be them.

The next time you find yourself judging someone—and you will, because we are imperfect humans—ask yourself to look deeper into why. You might just learn something about what's going on inside of you.

The rest of our meeting was great. We had a ton in common, and although we are fourteen years apart, we had very similar views on music and the industry. It was a refreshing conversation, and by the time our appetizers were gone we were laughing like old friends. Terry began to steer the conversation back toward the purpose of the meeting and asked me when I could start.

I was confused. I thought we were going to build a duo and start from there. So when he asked me again when I could start practicing with the guys, I stopped him and said, "I'm sorry, I missed a step. What guys?"

"The Clients," he said. "We want you to be the female lead of The Clients."

He went on to explain that they were restructuring the band because their piano player was retiring as of the first of the year. He had already hired a young piano player named Kyle who was set to start the first of the year, and I would round out the new format.

I'm pretty sure that's what he said anyway… I was hearing him, but I was so excited that I could barely sit still. First of all, The Clients were one of the most well-known bands in the area and had been playing together for years. Secondly, they were a working band, meaning I would have a job. And last but not least, things were coming full circle for me. The Clients were the same band that my ex paid to get me on stage with in my early twenties. The funny thing about that full circle experience is that I was in such a dark place that I didn't even realize just how special and significant that really was. Sometimes I think we do that—fail to see blessings because we are so clouded by our struggles. It's something I try to practice daily now, seeing the blessing instead of the struggle, but at that time I just didn't see how cool this really was. It is one of my favorite stories to tell now.

Practice was going to be on Thursday nights at Kyle's house. We had a few months to get our show together before the changing of the guard in January. It was early November now, so that didn't give us much time. Charlie was doing a little better, so I figured we could give it a trial run with him staying home with the kids when I went to practice and on show nights, and then I would stay home with the kids during the day. At this point having me out of the house while he was home was better for everyone, so he seemed content with the plan.

Practice was great. I instantly felt at home with the band and they were a fun group of guys. I could tell they hadn't had a girl around much, and it wasn't long before I adapted and fell into being just one of the guys. Terry is very old-fashioned, and because he brought me into the band, I think he felt responsible in some way for me. So when one of the guys jokingly made an offhanded or pervy comment, Terry would reprimand them like a dad and we would all laugh. All but Terry, that is. He was very much the dad of the group. We affectionately call him Uncle Terry even now. Our friendship within the band grew quickly, and before we knew it we were all like family. I'd like to think that I brought in a little sensitivity and sentiment by making sure they all realized how lucky we were to have each other, but I think they all secretly knew that already.

One night about halfway through practice my phone rang. It was Heather, and I figured she just wanted to chat, but as soon as the phone stopped ringing it started again. I excused myself from practice and took the call. She was in my driveway and had come to pick up her son, who had been at my house with Daniel, and she said that she didn't know what to do because Charlie was inside with the baby and didn't seem coherent. *Son of a...here we go again.*

I told the guys I had an emergency and I had to go. So I left practice and drove home. Charlie was in his slurring/not slurring stage again, and my heart sank.

After everyone was asleep, I was sitting up thinking about what my next step should be when my cell phone rang. It was Terry. He was worried about me and was wondering what happened.

I broke down. It was embarrassing and unprofessional, but I couldn't stop myself. I told him everything between sniffles and throat clearing, and I completely unloaded all of my personal baggage into the receiver of the phone. Whew...that was *a lot* of information. The other end of the phone was quiet for a few seconds, and I assumed that he was trying to think of ways to tell me I was fired because the band didn't have time for drama like this. But instead, like someone had taken his breath away, he simply said, "Wow. I am so sorry." Then he asked me a question I will never forget. It was a simple question with few words, but it was so impactful that it stopped me in my tracks. He said, "What do we do now?"

Not "you're fired" or "what are *you* going to do now?" or "danger, danger, this girl is crazy!" Nope. None of these things.

"What do we do now", and from that moment on I didn't feel alone anymore.

The first few shows with The Clients were rough. We had been practicing and we sounded tight, so that wasn't the problem. The issue started when some of the band's female following was less than thrilled to see "their band" with a new female lead singer. This was not something I had anticipated. I had been in bands for a few years now and on the music scene for most of my twenties, and although the music industry in our area was predominantly men, most of the women I had met through the music biz had been supportive. This was different.

I suppose as with any other band there are fans who feel a sort of ownership or are slightly possessive. We see this sometimes when a smaller band with a cult-type following hits the big time and they actually lose fans because their original followers feel as if the band sold out, when actually they're just taking the next step in their career.

Anyway, The Clients had some of these women, so when I stepped off the stage after our first show, grateful for the opportunity, I was completely blindsided by a woman who actually pulled my hair out of my ponytail holder and said, "There, that's better. If you're going to be in a band you should probably stop dressing like a teacher." Crickets. No words. I'm not about confrontation, like I told you earlier, so I just stood there dumbfounded at what had just happened.

During the next show, on one of our breaks a woman actually backed me into a corner and put her finger in my face and asked, "Who the hell do you think you are?" Yet another time I actually got locked in a bathroom with a woman who demanded that I quit. Pack that onto a group of bandmates who loving but relentlessly liked to tease me (they still do this, but I have started jokingly telling them that I may or may not be slowly poisoning them; I think they're actually a little nervous, so it's slowed down), and finally a marriage that was on its last leg, and I started to lose weight. Fast. My stomach was in tight knots at all times and I couldn't eat more than a few bites before everything in my GI tract started seizing up and cramping.

Now don't get me wrong. For every mean girl, there was usually a tribe of strong, beautiful, happy women who lifted me up and supported me from day one. Nine times out of ten those women were somehow associated with Lois Darlington.

Lois is the owner of Clayton's Tap. Clayton's is where I met Terry and sang with the band for the first time. It is also the first venue where I played as an official member with the band. It would go on to become the cornerstone of my musical career and the roots of where I began writing again, a place I will always call home.

Clayton's Tap serves as the backdrop for every milestone in our lives. Anything we have celebrated, announced, said goodbye to, or welcomed seems to have taken place on a stage in the back room of Clayton's. It is the venue that every band wants to play in this area, and when we sometimes forget how far we've come, all we have to do is look around at the walls that are adorned with our band pictures and, most recently, canvas prints of our original lyrics.

Lois is more like a sister to me than a friend. She welcomed me into her large Irish family almost immediately. She has a brilliant mind and can function on hardly any sleep so well that she doesn't miss a beat. She has a head full of thick auburn hair that is almost as fiery as her laugh, and her drive is so fierce you either try to keep up with her or get run over by her fury. Her love of humankind is evident in the way she can bring a group of strangers together and watch them walk away as forever friends. She is classy and savvy and can navigate downtown Chicago like she's the mayor. She might actually be the mayor—it wouldn't shock us.

Lois rocks a full-time career in Chicago alongside powerful businessmen and women in a competitive and cutting-edge industry and hops on the train that takes her sixty miles southwest to get home on the daily. She raises a family and *still* manages to run Clayton's Tap. She can kick your ass in heels or in a hoodie and she will look like a million bucks doing it.

The group of women she calls friends were almost instantly by my side as well. These are the kind of women you want in your tribe. They come from all walks of life and all sorts of career paths but the thread they all have in common is simple. Humility.

You're sick? They put together a food train. You're

selling pies for your sixth grader's school fundraiser? They buy them all. You're the new girl in a band standing on a stage looking terrified? They stand in front and dance and cheer and make you feel like you're P!nk. Quite honestly it's because of this group that I didn't quit after that first show.

By the time I had done a dozen or so shows with The Clients, I was getting tired of watching tables of women smirk and whisper behind hands held to their mouths. I knew they were talking about me. I could feel it. Now, some of this may have actually been the paranoia I was driven to out of sheer insecurity, but whenever I didn't have my Lois tribe with me, I felt like a lone survivor.

It would affect my performance. I was such a nervous wreck from absorbing the energy that some of these women put out that I was afraid to be myself. That frustrated me to no end, considering I now encourage and teach people to never dim their light.

Every show while setting up I would feel eyes on me. Many nights there would be a table of women trying to figure out who I was. Were they all mean? I don't know if that's a fair statement, but in my mind they were. For all I know they could have been talking about how the venue changed its lighting, but the second they pointed in my direction I was sure as ever that they were talking about me.

I came up with a plan. I figured that if I was nice to them, then they would have no choice but to be nice back. So I would take in a deep breath of bravery, walk tall and steady to their table, and say, "Hi Ladies, my name is Jonelle. I'm with the band. Is there anything you would like to hear tonight? Oh and by the way, I love those shoes/that purse/your jewelry/your shirt/your total resting bitch face looking me up and down and making me squirm in my shoes." Stuff like that.

And second by second the table of once unapproachable women were in the palm of my hand.

"Sure, we can do some Carrie Underwood for you. Oh yes, I love that song too." And you know what? By the time the night was over, they were dancing and singing along to their new friend, the band girl. And when I would give them a little attention from the stage with a point or a wink, you would have thought that I was superwoman. Not only that, but guess who kept coming to shows? Mission accomplished.

This might not be the best lesson to teach if you are only looking at the exterior of it all. We most likely don't want to teach our daughters to be fake or to kiss ass to be liked. That is not at all why I was doing this. What I was actually doing was turning the tables so that I was in control of the situation. If I approached a table with confidence and grace, then I gained respect for myself and from others. Once you feel respected and you equally respect others, it feels safe to shine.

Between navigating new friendships, a new job, and learning how to be the front woman of a working band, I was starting to feel quite a bit of anxiety. Sometimes I felt like I had been dropped into someone else's life. Some days I liked it, some days it made me uneasy. Looking back I can see that my life was changing at such a rapid rate that most days I was uncomfortable, but like they say, you have to get uncomfortable to grow. It must be uncomfortable to burst from a seed and push up through the cold, hard soil to become a healthy blade of grass, but without the discomfort you are still just a seed hidden deep down in the ground far away from the sunlight.

On September first, two days before my thirtieth birthday, I told Charlie I wanted a divorce. A month later he moved into an apartment in the downtown district. Interestingly, his drinking slowed and he was actually a fun-loving father. A few months after our divorce, he lost his job. Although it was a bad time for him financially, he was able to spend a lot of time with Marley, which helped me a lot when I would go to work. I didn't have to pay for childcare, and that made a huge difference.

Let's briefly visit my thirtieth birthday. Terry decided to throw me a party. It was a very sweet gesture and all of our band family was there. My birthday always lands around Labor Day, so we actually had a few days of things lined up to do as a group. The kids were with their dads and I found myself with three whole days alone, so it was a welcome invitation to hang with my new friends for the weekend. Day one we went to a Doobie Brothers concert, day two a ball game, and day three we celebrated my birthday.

It had been a very fun but long three days, and around 10 p.m. just as the party was really getting started, I looked around the room and realized that I didn't really know anyone. I mean, yes, I knew them, but I didn't really *know* know them. I suddenly felt completely alone in a group of people as the realization of my divorce started to hit me, right there at 10 p.m. at a party for me in a group of friendly strangers. I don't know if I have felt sadness or loneliness at that level again.

I knew that I was making the right decision to leave, but I still had to mourn the loss of a marriage, a home shared with someone, as difficult as it had been on some days. Dreams and hopes signed away on a few lines in the courthouse. Divorce is a very sad situation, and even when it's necessary, it can be an extremely dark time.

I drove home that night and pulled right up to a road block. My insurance card was old, so the officer had to give me a ticket. I remember looking at him with tears in my eyes as I said, "I'm 30 today, and I am getting divorced," in a sad realization how life was changing so quickly.

He said, "Ma'am, I'm sorry you're having a bad day, but I have to give you a ticket." And just like that, life reminded me that even when it hurts like hell, not everyone is going to give you a break. *Dear God, please make forty more fun than this…* And oh how He did.

Chapter 8
The One You Need

A FEW MONTHS INTO MY DIVORCE, on a sticky summer night, a couple of the guys and I stayed after to tear down and load out, and then we sat outside on the hood of one of our cars sipping on a cold beer. This wasn't the first time we had been the last few to leave. It didn't take long to figure out that these few guys were in the same boat as me. They were in marriages that were not going to work out. At one point, four of the six members were going through a divorce. I joke when telling that story that we were the worst band in the world to hire for weddings that year, but really we were just a foursome of lost souls. Our sound guy quickly started dating someone, so he was the first to leave the lonely hearts club, leaving only three of us and Kyle, who was young enough to still stay out all night.

Weekend after weekend we would leave the venue and go for a pontoon ride or meet up for a truck stop breakfast.

Sometimes we would sit on the tailgate of a truck on a country road and watch the horizon turn from a deep, dark black to a navy blue and finally to a purple-pink haze—our signal that we should all go our separate ways and get some sleep. When you don't have anyone to go home to, it's easy to just not go home.

As sad as those times could be they were also some of the best times of my life. We were just three people, silently releasing our pain into the night sky until the break of dawn would shed a comforting glow on us, reminding us that it is truly darkest before the dawn.

It wasn't until Terry had moved down the street into his new apartment that we started to recognize our friendship had grown into more. It wasn't the fact that he moved literally footsteps away from me, or that we had so much in common that our "oh my gosh, me too" conversations were starting to get sickening. It was the way we both felt like we were home in each other's presence that found us having a late-night conversation of realization.

This wasn't a storybook Disney princess and a lost shoe kind of moment. No, not at all. It was more of a terrifying moment that neither of us could deny. Terrifying because we were both just barely on the other side of ending relationships—long-term, years-of-work-and-commitment, four-kids-involved, bare-wire-emotions kind of relationships. Terrifying because we were both severely broken. Terrifying because it didn't affect just us but families and friends and an entire band full of people who were counting on us. Terrifying because we both desperately needed to be loved for who we were—and we were both so sure that we were unlovable.

In every sense this should have been a disaster, and believe me when I tell you that there were days when it was as if a bomb had detonated. But somehow, at the end of the day, no matter how ugly, dark, stressful, anxiety-ridden, and scary it was, somehow we still found ourselves exhaling and more than anything...home.

Around the time when Charlie moved out, it became apparent that I was going to need to get a second job. I applied at Morris Hospital and was hired as a patient care tech for the new immediate care that had just been built. I was excited to get back into health care. I had held a few odd jobs in the medical field throughout the years and had been able to keep up my CNA through doing some home health with Pepere. Also, Terry was going to nursing school, and I was seriously thinking about it too. It was a complicated and long process to actually get hired, so I was thrilled when my first day at the hospital was approaching.

Have you ever walked into a room and felt like you have been there before? Like a comforting déjà vu experience? That's what I felt when I walked into Ridge Road. That's what we called our campus because, well, it was on Ridge Road. The team I was going to be working with was made up of another tech, five nurses, an imaging staff, a lab tech, a nurse practitioner, a physician assistant, and a few docs.

The physician on duty changed daily, but for the most part I was on the same schedule as the nurses who were working the day I started. Nicky, our other tech, worked opposite me, and although she and I ended up dear friends, we never did get the opportunity to work hand in hand. I *loved* this staff. We were like a little family.

Some of my favorite friends are the friends I met while working at Ridge Road. We worked twelve-hour shifts, and on slow days we had time to really get to know each other. My sweet friend Julie was one of the best nurses I've ever known. She was gracious and warm and hilarious. She called everyone "lovey" and made delicious-smelling homemade sugar hand scrub that she gave away as gifts in little tiny mason jars. Her stories were so random and unbelievable that you couldn't have made them up. She followed the Grateful Dead for a while and met her husband, Bill, in Alabama when they were just kids. She and Bill got divorced, remarried, and then divorced again, so she affectionately nicknamed him "Rex" for re-ex.

Julie made everything fun. Have to clean up poop? Julie made some sort of poop game out of it that had us cracking up and trying to not get ourselves in trouble with our strict, by-the-book boss. Her ideas were clever and silly; although it was never approved at our monthly morning meeting, she tried like hell to introduce a "knock your socks off" reward, where everyone in the department would donate a pair of silly socks, and when someone went above and beyond and "knocked your socks off" they would get to pick a pair out of the basket. Brilliant, if you ask me.

Julie was one of the most caring nurses to her patients, implementing her nursing skills effortlessly, and her patients loved her. She made them all feel like royalty. Jules—one of my favorite people on the planet.

By the time I was working at Ridge Road I had put in a few years with the band, but I was starting to miss writing. I had tossed around the idea of doing a separate original project, but we just didn't have the time or the material I needed. So I worked at the hospital in the day and on the weekends I played music.

My relationship with Terry had flourished into a fully committed partnership. We had endured plenty of bumps in the road with our kids and exes, but all in all people seemed genuinely happy for us. We both were just so happy, and our friends, family, and fans could see it. We were careful with how we crossed our on-stage life with our personal life, so it never became a problem. Something about starting off as coworkers and friends first seemed to set that standard. It's easy for us to turn it on and off and be present where we are.

I am a huge supporter of couples working together. I know it can get tricky and it doesn't work for everyone, but when two entrepreneurs share the same vision it kind of becomes their baby, and that is what our first album would eventually become. Our baby.

We were also dealing with a tough financial situation. Divorce isn't cheap, and post-divorce is even more expensive. Between Terry's child support going out for his two children, none coming in for Marley, attorney fees, childcare (I was working full time again, so off to daycare we go), and paying for two homes, we decided that our next move would be just that—to move in together. Just typing that makes me breathe fast, but not because I wasn't ready or we didn't have a great relationship. Because when you get divorced and your dad comes over to help you repaint your walls to cover the memories they bring back, and you're just starting to fall into a new system and schedule… Well, the thought of moving out and in with another man comes with a little anxiety. Oh yeah, and I still had a toddler. So there was that.

We talked numbers and ideas and fears and excitement. We loaded up the car with a diaper bag and extra snacks and sippy cups and drove a thirty-mile radius looking at neighborhoods and towns. We stopped at empty homes that were for sale and peered into windows. We walked through a few we knew we couldn't afford but dreamt about it anyway.

We finally decided to sit down and talk to a builder in a growing subdivision just west of town. It was new construction and they offered a variety of options to buy, which seemed to fit our financial situation best. Because it was new construction, we had a lot of options and choices. We finally settled on a large ranch duplex plan that would include three bedrooms, a Jack and Jill-style bathroom, a master suite with a walk-in closet and a master bath, a large open living space with a shared kitchen and dining room plan, a large laundry room off of the two-car garage, and a full unfinished basement.

Next thing we knew, we were picking out tile and countertops, and before long we were painting our kitchen on scaffolding to reach the tops of the walls against the cathedral ceilings. Breadbasket. That was the color of our kitchen. A warm rusty brown.

I know it sounds fishy that we were both dealing with financial situations yet were able to build a home, but when we put our finances together, we were better off together than we were alone, much like everything else we would do. But would this prove to be enough? Could we live on small paychecks and big love? Time would tell...

Moving in together was an easy transition. We were already much like a family. Terry has a daughter and a son, both around the same age as Daniel. We were an instant family of six, pulling chairs up to one of our kitchen tables and crunching in two adults and four kids, including a high chair on weekends when we had all of our children. We both craved normalcy in terms of having a safe place to land for us and for our children. We were a broken family in every sense of the term. My children had two different fathers, Terry's children had a mother with a spoken agenda to ruin him.

I laugh when I look back at the first few holiday photos. Awkward ages and awkward emotions plagued the three older kids something awful, but the love was big. We all loved each other from the start. There was, surprisingly, never much if any anger from the older kids. There were emotions, don't get me wrong, but our little family was a safe place to land, and so began my mission to make our home the family safe space. The place where the kids could come any time and get a hot meal, a warm bed to sleep in, laughter, love, and a sense of belonging. This mission would break my heart over and over throughout the years when real life would rear its ugly head.

Terry tends to lean toward the glass-is-half-empty way of thinking and is easily discouraged, so when things like holidays didn't work in our favor for having all of the kids, he would see my disappointment and in turn create a Chicken Little effect. The sky was falling—until it wasn't, and we would take a deep breath and start over. This is still our pattern today. If one of us starts going down, the other one follows close behind. Healthy? Probably not. True? You bet.

Moving out of the duplex I had lived in with Charlie was cleansing. I was still trying to muster enough strength to physically move things out, but every time I walked into that duplex it was as if the energy sucked me dry. So when the U-Haul pulled in and I didn't have the basement even close to organized for moving because it was full of Charlie's unwanted stuff, my friend and fellow musician Greg looked me square in the eye and told me to, "Get outta here for a while. I've got this." And he moved everything in my basement up and out.

Greg isn't sensitive, or at least I didn't think he was. He is a hard-working, no nonsense guy who loves beer, drums, and cars. He has been through a thing or two in his own life, so I think he sympathized with me when he saw me simply staring into crates full Charlie's junk. Junk because not even Charlie wanted it. So Greg got down to business and loaded up a dumpster and a U-Haul, and when I returned home later that day, he matter-of-factly told me that it was all done. Something I will never forget.

Terry's apartment was a different story. He had only been there around a year, and it had been a place of peace for us. Being in my duplex was awkward for him since there was still so much of Charlie left, so we spent a lot of time at his place. It was a simple second floor, two bedroom, one-and-a-half bath apartment with a little bitty balcony that faced the highway. It was built in the '60s and had not been updated much, so the bathtub clogged up with every shower, requiring an ungodly amount of Drano. Still, it was peaceful.

We learned a lot about ourselves and each other in that apartment. When we would feel like we each needed some space, I would walk home to my duplex. When I felt like I couldn't be alone, he would drive over to my house and sit with me until I fell asleep. He learned that I was serious about having terrible motion sickness after a spontaneous ride on the county fair Tilt-A-Whirl landed me in bed for two days. I learned that he requires more sleep than I ever do.

We left our band jobs in the wee hours of the morning, and instead of sitting outside watching sunrises with friends, we sat on his hand-me-down couch and ate ramen noodles and peanut butter sandwiches. He had lost everything in his divorce, only coming out on the other side with his clothes, a few guitars, a bucket of cleaning supplies, and his prized stereo, which he would eventually have to sell to pay the lawyer. This was the real definition of money not making you happy. We didn't have much in those years, but we had each other.

As we were emptying boxes in the garage a few weeks after moving into our new duplex, a booming voice shouted, "Knock knock!" which made us both jump. There was one duplex to the east of ours and empty lots surrounding us on every other side, so we were surprised to hear another voice. A large man with messy gray hair who looked like he could be a distant relative of Johnny Cash appeared in the garage. He had warm eyes and a gruff voice with a South Side Chicago accent that sputtered out words like "tree" instead of "three".

His name was Art, and he was a truck driver who lived in the duplex next door with his partner, Sandy. We would go on to be like family with Art and Sandy until we lost Art a few short years later to cancer. We didn't get him for very long, but his impact on our lives was forever. One of our favorite songs, "Angel Eyes", that would eventually go on our first album was written about Art. We wrote it before he passed and let him hear it in its simple form before it was ever finished. We didn't tell him it was about him, just let him listen.

"Ride, cowboy, ride till you reach that mountain high, and you see your angel eyes, she'll be waiting for you. And you can fly, cowboy, fly, reach on up and touch the sky until you ride, cowboy, ride with your angel eyes".

He died a few short months later. We know he is riding high with his angel eyes and looking over us every day. When we are especially missing him all we have to do is close our eyes and count one, two, tree...and he is there.

During our time living in the new duplex and during our time prior to that, the band was playing fairly steadily until of one the guys started a new job, and not long after, another one of the guys did too. This created a little tension because it was only going to allow us to play on Saturday nights instead of any time. Terry, Kyle, and I were the three members who relied on the band income as part of our household income and not side money, so we were going to take an even greater hit with the band's reduced availability.

I had been tossing around the idea in my head of doing something with original music, and it seemed like this change in schedule was finally going to give me the opportunity to pitch the idea to Terry. Since it was a way to keep us working, he agreed but remained a little leery about the idea of doing all original music, especially since we didn't have any written other than my first album and a couple of just okay singles that had dropped in between then and now. He felt like maybe I was putting the cart before the horse. Which, I will admit, I tend to do.

I don't look at this as a negative; in fact, it's how I accomplish almost all of my goals. Don't have original songs for the new original band? Better get writing then. You can apply that to anything you're trying to accomplish. It is called—we're back to that word from earlier, remember it? Say it with me: manifesting.

So we manifested and set intentions and manifested some more, and pretty soon this new idea was not only rolling but brought completely to life. With a few exceptions. We were going to have to start with cover music and revisit the idea of originals when we actually had some. But for now, the band would start only with covers.

Sometimes you have to bend a little in order to experience the full reward. I am reminding myself about this point just as much as I am reminding you. It is one of the things I am working on. Bending.

We also knew that we needed to include Kyle on this journey. His income was also going to be affected, and he would need to replace it. Plus his piano playing is beyond anything we've ever heard. It rounded out Terry's picking style nicely, plus he could sing, so win-win. We ran the idea of this acoustic trio by him and he was immediately interested. So we ran into the studio to make a quick demo, and two days later we booked our first job. Yep, you heard me. We—well, maybe I—booked our first job and it was going to be in two weeks. We didn't even have a name. Oh no, this was just like Dead Man Drag but worse!

I took to social media and started asking for ideas for an acoustic band name that was organic and fit the country feel we had. We all had country roots. Kyle had played in a well-known Central Illinois country band for a few years, Terry was raised by a country guitar picker and had lived in Nashville and toured with country star Sammy Kershaw, and I had been brought up listening to all kinds of music, but country is what stuck to my bones like good old smoked ribs and sauce. See? Told you we think country.

One by one people weighed in with their ideas. We led them a little with a post asking for names that included words like creek, stream, river, or grass. We had all kinds of weigh-ins. Some serious, some funny, some (mostly from other musicians) totally out there. Finally, a friend, a fellow musician in our community, typed this: "Hey, how about River Road?" And it just seemed to click. I had grown up near a River Road, Kyle's mom had too, and Terry passed a River Road sign every day on his way to work. There were River Roads everywhere. So just like that, we picked our name. River Road Trio.

Our first show was at The Lantern on the riverwalk in downtown Naperville. Since we hadn't written anything yet, we planned on playing three sets of covers. We arrived a few hours early to set up, and when starting time came around we were face to face with a table of two people who were just about done eating their dinner. We played a few songs and the nice people gave us a thumbs up and threw a five into our tip jar. Mostly out of pity, I'm sure, because we were totally lost. We were basically playing The Clients' set list without a drummer or bass player. To the unsuspecting ear I'm sure we were fine, but to us we were tanking...and fast.

After that first show, we decided we needed an entirely new set list. We came up with three lists of ideas, put them together, and had a few rehearsals. We also did a quick photo shoot for promo purposes and set out again to book more jobs.

We played The Lantern a few more times until the general manager and our contact magically disappeared into thin air. That's something we're used to in the music industry. Don't ever get too comfortable with the way things are set up because I assure you, they will change in the blink of an eye. Just like the time we tried to open the door to set up at a venue and it was locked—the whole place was closed down. Or the time that the once rowdy crowd who loved our music had turned into an early bird special crowd, and we were asked to turn it down so many times that we actually turned off our speakers and just let the jukebox play.

I wish I could tell you the number of times we have played to practically no one. I wish you could see the years of paid practice we got. Hey, better than looking at it in a negative way! I wish you could understand the pull that national sports teams have over almost everyone in Chicagoland, making it almost impossible to find a venue that doesn't offer TV-lined bars and walls stacked top to bottom, side to side with sports channels and games, stealing everyone's attention from the stage (or the tiny section of floor next to the popcorn machine that was called a stage) and us playing to the backs of people's heads. I wish you could see what the room looks like at 2 a.m. when the venue is closed and the smoke and mirrors of the stage and the night have been replaced with fluorescent overhead lights, and the smell of cologne and beer has been replaced with bleach water as the late shift cleans up. Yet here we are, over a decade later, wrapping cables while making small talk with the closing bartenders and counting tips as the adrenaline needed to get through a show fades from our now tired bodies. I can assure you, as long as I can help it, I will never have another job other than this.

One night while we were sitting on our couch after the kids were in bed, Terry was noodling on the guitar like he always is. People ask us all the time if we walk around our house singing and playing guitar, and the answer is absolutely we do.

So it's just a regular night, and he's playing something I have never heard when all of the sudden the chords that he was strumming made me sit up a little taller and cock my head to the side.

"Play that again," I said. So he did and I heard it again. A lyric in my head. I ran to get paper and jotted down what I had heard, and we continued on strumming and jotting and strumming and jotting. After three minutes of jotting down lyrics, excitement welled up in my chest.

"Listen," I said. So he played the chords and I sang the lyrics on the paper, and when we finished we both sat quietly smiling.

"Let's call it 'Lucky'," I said. And that is the story of how our very first single to ever hit the airwaves was born.

After "Lucky" the floodgates opened, and "Bar Room Walls", "The Pitcher", and a song that we have yet to record called "Home" were born, followed by a few more ideas. Some were developed into complete songs, some are still left hanging in time, patiently waiting for someone to open their pages and finish their stories. Some came to life on napkins or the back of a receipt, some on the many blank pages of journals given to me as gifts throughout the years. But one song would live in limbo and not find its ending for more than two years, finally going on to find its purpose eight years later. "The One You Need" has a story behind it that brings me to my knees and a story in front of it that no one could have ever written.

While showering after a late show and recapping the night, a lyric popped into my head. I wish there were a more romantic description complete with wine and candles, but I was literally shaving my legs and lathering up with whatever Bath and Body Works shower gel had made it onto the shower shelf when a lyric, like magic, appeared in my head. Sometimes this Houdini stuff is exhausting. *Really bad timing, song! I need to sleep!* But when it hits me, it hits me.

Sometimes I have to figure out the mystery of the scene unfolding before me. If I hear, "He watched her standing in the mirror as the truth was getting clearer, the day before seemed better than today." I'm thinking, *Hmmm nothing yet.* I replay it over and over, and then, "He said, 'Now I'm the one who's stronger, you can't hide it any longer, so close your eyes and I'll take your pain away.'" *Okay, I see... She must be ill. Seriously ill. She just found out. It's cancer. He has to be strong for her now because she is just too tired.*

"I'll be your eyes when you can't see. I'll be the strength you need to get up off your knees. I'll be your breath when you can't breathe. You've been the one, now it's time for me to be the one you need." *Ah, I see. The chorus is the message.*

He is going to perform the ultimate task of love and be what she needs because she can't right now. She just can't.

This is where the song ended and where it stayed for two years, because three weeks later we found ourselves in the leading roles of this imaginary movie. The characters in the song suddenly became us—I was her and Terry was him. This boulder rolled us right over, and by the time the dust settled, I was the one saying, "I just can't right now. I just can't."

I had cancer.

Chapter 9
I Still Do

CANCER IS ONE OF THOSE words that is borderline profanity. Think about it. Profanity can make people uncomfortable, and the word "cancer" makes many people uncomfortable. It's a dirty little word, but unlike slipping up and using some explicit language, the word cancer can actually hurt you. It brings a whole new level to the saying "sticks and stones can break my bones but words can never hurt me." Trust me, they can.

The first question people ask me when this subject comes up and I tell someone that I had cancer is, "How did you know you had it?" Because I have asked this question myself, I know that they're asking partly because they are curious and partly because they are hoping for an answer that reassures them they don't have it.

I had noticed a new pain in my throat when I would sing for too long. It was a sharp, stabbing pain that was deep and would increase when I took in a breath. It would make me stand frozen like a statue until it faded away. This, however, was not what made me finally make an appointment with my doctor.

I had been experiencing headaches for a few weeks in the same exact spot around my hairline. My aunt had a brain tumor a few years prior, and I was convinced that I had one too. My doctor knew my worry, so he ordered blood work and a CT scan of my brain. When the results came in, everything looked okay except for one thing. My calcium was high. I figured this was because I had been working out and drinking some smoothies and had increased my dairy consumption, but upon further investigation my blood work came back with a high level of PTH.

PTH is the parathyroid hormone that regulates serum calcium in the body. When high levels are present, it usually indicates a benign parathyroid tumor. The parathyroid glands actually have zero to do with the thyroid but live right behind it in the body. So because of the blood work, I was referred to an endocrinologist who then set me up for an ultrasound of the neck. During that ultrasound, a tumor was found and later biopsied by a fine needle biopsy.

Now, if you have had thyroid problems, you are probably well aware of fine needle biopsies. If you have not had thyroid issues, then let me explain this oh so relaxing procedure. You are fully awake and not sedated in the slightest. You lay on a procedure table and a radiologist, a nurse, a rad tech, and a pathologist are in the room. The radiologist begins by asking you to lie perfectly still, no talking or swallowing. Have you ever tried not to swallow after someone tells you not to? It's like trying not to blink while someone comes at your eye. Darn near impossible. While another member of the medical team holds the ultrasound wand to your neck, the radiologist uses a long, thin needle to administer a local anesthesia into the area he or she will be working in. Once "numb" the radiologist uses another long, fine needle to pull out tiny samples of the tumor for testing. That is where pathology takes the field. The radiologist drops the samples onto a slide, and the pathologist looks under a microscope to make sure there is enough tissue to be sent off for testing. Once it's over, they give you a Band-Aid and an ice pack and you're all set. Not the worst thing I have ever had done but definitely not the best.

I was just pulling out of the driveway to head to Sam's Club with Terry when the endocrinologist called. This is how I remember the conversation:

"Your biopsy came back, and it *is* cancer, so we're diagnosing you with two things. Hyperparathyroidism and thyroid cancer."

Whoa. "Okay, let me pull over and throw the car into park before we have this talk." But she went on.

"If you are going to have cancer, this is the best kind to have".

Okay…I didn't realize there could be a "best" cancer to have.

"It's called papillary carcinoma, and it's cancer of the thyroid. Easy to treat…" She went on, but I stopped listening for a second. I was watching a bird walk on its two little crooked legs, trying to cross the road in front of me, its perfect feathers ruffled up as it found a puddle from an early morning storm. The warm afternoon sun turned up the late summer humidity. It occurred to me how ironic it was that outside of the car was a picture perfect day, and inside of the car everything was crashing down around me.

"Make an appointment with me for two weeks from today." And a few seconds later, we hung up.

I'm not sure I can forget the look on Terry's face when I said, "She said it *is* cancer." He was so painfully crushed.

I read everything I could find and soaked in everything I could about papillary carcinoma. Just as I started to think I had a good understanding of this disease, the phone rang again.

Apparently the hospital sent off the biopsied tissue to a second lab for confirmation, and when the second lab report came back it had conflicting information. It didn't seem to show papillary carcinoma and, as a matter of fact, it didn't even show thyroid cancer at all. It definitely showed carcinoma of some sort, but the cells didn't look like something they had seen before.

"Huh."

No, really. All I could say was, "Huh."

This is when the endocrinologist broke up with me. She hadn't seen these types of cells and wanted to be sure I had the right care. She said, "It's me, not you...but actually, it's you." Okay, she didn't say that, but it felt like it.

So up to Loyola I went. She had made me an appointment with an endocrine surgeon, Dr. Steven DeJong, one of the top surgeons at Loyola University Medical Center.

Dr. DeJong is a clinical expert in endocrine disease and parathyroid disorders. He is also a general surgeon professor, which means he teaches medical students while carrying a patient load and intense surgical cases. He is basically brilliant and highly respected by his patients and fellow physicians, which could only mean one thing: I was going to be terrified of him.

You see, I have this tiny little thing called an authority figure fear, and this authoritative figure was keeping me up at night in preparation for my first appointment. But a few days before I was supposed to be there, I got a phone call from Loyola.

I figured it was going to be one of those automated messages reminding me of my upcoming appointment, but when I answered the call, there was a real live human on the other end. That human's name was Nadine, and she was Dr. DeJong's nurse practitioner. She would go on to become one of the most important people in my world and one of my dearest friends. That first phone call from Nadine changed everything for me. She said to me, and I quote, "I know this is scary, but you've got me now."

A few days later I got to put a face with the name, and she hugged me tightly when we met. Honestly, there wasn't much of a choice after that. Both of us knew we would be forever friends.

Let me explain the way things work at a teaching hospital. As you know, I'm better with talking about things in terms of food. A teaching hospital is like a four-course meal. The nurse is the appetizer, the nurse practitioner is the salad course, the med student is the main course, and finally the physician rounds out your meal with the perfect finishing touches. The physician is dessert, and Dr. Steven DeJong was the sweetest thing I had ever met.

"There she is," he said in an upbeat tone while walking into the exam room. I stood to shake his hand, and the first thing I noticed was a Mickey Mouse pin on the breast of his white lab coat. There was something about the pin that put me at ease. Here is this highly trained and educated professional who isn't afraid to show his childlike side.

Dr. DeJong, Terry, a med student, and I discussed the lab results and the possibilities of what he believed it could be and what some of our options were. Surgery was inevitable, but what would take place during surgery was the big question. Dr. DeJong wanted to go over some more labs that would be drawn there and sent to the Loyola lab, and I would meet with a scheduling liaison to find a date for surgery. We settled on September 6, 2011.

Once our initial appointment was over, Terry and I drove to Mon Ami Gabi, a classic French bistro in Oakbrook. We took stress eating to a whole new level, ordering brie cheese with honey, roasted garlic, and toasted hazelnuts piled high on crusty crostini; croque monsieur; soup du jour; sparkling white wine; and a trio of chocolate mousses with a café Gabi. We ate like kings and would turn this dining experience into a tradition every year at checkup time.

On Saturday, September 3 I turned thirty-three years old. It was Labor Day weekend, and we had two shows with The Clients. I was happy to be playing two nights in a row because after surgery I was going to have to take about six weeks off. Plus, music heals me in every way possible, and since I was anxious about surgery, I was happy to be able to take my mind off things for at least a little while.

After our Saturday night show, Terry asked me if I wanted to take a ride to our spot. Our spot was the place where he kissed me for the first time after a night of unexpected events that led us to sitting silently in the car listening to Steve Earle's "The Galway Girl". The place where we first talked about our feelings for each other changing, along with the fear of losing a friendship, overridden by the fear of not expressing ourselves. Our spot wasn't much of a sight to see, but it was special to us. He knew that I was emotional and knew exactly where to take me.

We pulled in, rolled down the windows, and shut the car's engine off, leaving nothing but the sound of cicadas singing and a frog somewhere in the distance. We reclined our seats, took a few cleansing post-show breaths, and sat silently in the quiet. My eyes were closed, but I could feel eyes on me, so I peeked to make sure it was still Terry. He was staring at me with a look I had never seen before. It was so serious that I pulled my seat back up and asked him if everything was okay.

He took my face in his hands and ran his thumbs over my cheeks, then my nose, then my forehead, and finally my lips, a move that he had made quite often, learning and remembering every curve, bump, and contour of my face. He was still looking deeply into my eyes when he reached into his pocket, pulled out a diamond ring, and asked me to marry him.

Two nights before surgery we played our annual Labor Day show at Clayton's Tap. It was such an emotional day with the excitement of everyone congratulating Terry and me on our engagement, and for a few moments I was able to forget that this was the last show I would perform before a surgical team would cut my throat open and move my vocal cords around. I remember this day like it happened this morning. Terry does too. In fact, he has a hard time talking about it.

As our fourth and final set came to a close, we said

our, "Goodnight, everybody, get home safe and thanks for coming out!" spiel. As the last cymbal crashes came raining down, it hit me out of nowhere all at once. I pointed my first finger up at the ceiling and twirled it in a fast circle, indicating that I wanted the band to keep going, to keep playing.

"Again, AGAIN!" I shouted over the crescendo that would lead to our big finish, but the energy of the music had everyone in their zone and they couldn't hear me. Tears were burning my already hot cheeks, and they kept coming as I kept trying to yell above the instruments.

Terry, trying not to look at me in order to keep it together himself, finally gave in and locked eyes with me. I mouthed half as a question and half in disbelief, "That's it?" just as the final snare hit fired off like a gun. Crash…and done. It was over. I think my soul knew more than I did that night, because it would be a very long journey back to that stage.

On this night I had a vivid dream. Dr. DeJong was sitting at a desk with a single lamp shining a dim light in a dark room. My point of view was from above looking down. I could see that he was frantically flipping pages of something important. As I looked a little closer, I could see that it was my chart. The look on his face was of pure determination. He was scanning each page like a speed reader, and although I can't explain it, I knew that he was learning fast. Solving a mystery. Figuring out what kind of cancer I had.

Two days later, he did exactly that.

Tuesday, September 6 came fast. Loyola is in Maywood, Illinois, a suburb of Chicago, and the traffic is no joke. Fall in Illinois is road construction season, and we were in the thick of it. Terry and I were chatting and joking around, trying to keep things light, but the heaviness in the car was hard to ignore. When we finally exited off of I55 onto 1st Avenue, our conversation went silent. Terry turned on the radio to try to break the quiet. Zac Brown and Jimmy Buffet sang about being "Knee Deep" in the water, and at one point at a red light, I seriously thought about getting out of the car to walk home. But as soon as the thought came into my head, the light turned green and we pulled into the hospital parking garage.

I need you to understand that I am going into so much detail during this part of the book because this is the part of my life when a pivotal change occurred. When I look back on the past, I categorize memories as before surgery and after surgery. These would be the last few hours I felt normal for a very long time. After surgery I had to learn a new normal, and although it wasn't a physical challenge, it was most definitely a mental challenge.

I have said it for eight years now: something changed when I went to sleep that day, and for a long time I fought like hell to get the old me back. It wasn't until recently that I started to understand that I was able to shed the old shell of myself and come out on the other side with a brand new set of wings.

Surgery was scheduled for 1 p.m. so we arrived around eleven to get registered and cross all of the T's and dot all of the I's. My parents and my aunt were in the surgical family waiting room when the registrar pointed us to where we would wait for the surgical nurse to come and get me. They were running behind and I was getting impatient, but I sat quietly spinning my newly placed engagement ring around my ring finger. My dad got up to go to the bathroom, and as soon as he disappeared around the corner, a nurse called my name. In a panic, I looked at my mom as if to say, "But Dad…" to which she said, "I'll tell him you went back."

The nurse walked Terry and me through a maze of fluorescent lit halls that led to a tiny room with a curtain instead of a door. Another nurse, who was straightening out IV tubing and squeezing a bag of saline, was waiting for us inside of the room. She gave us both a sunny hello and asked me to confirm my last name and date of birth. I was asked to change into a gown, blue slip-proof socks, and a disposable surgical cap, and even though I was given a few warm blankets, my body shook with nerves.

Once my IV was started, my medical history discussed, and the anesthesiologist stopped in for a quick visit, a familiar voice echoed through the halls.

"There she is," said Dr. DeJong. My body relaxed a little as he shook Terry's hand and pulled up a rolling stool. What he said next will never not blow my mind.

He said, "I have been going through your records and the lab results in your chart. I have gone over them multiple times, each time thoroughly, and I think I know what kind of cancer we're dealing with."

I wanted to shout, "Oh, doc, I know, I saw you. I watched you at your desk, pouring your heart into my chart. I *saw* you."

But instead I just nodded in understanding as he explained that they would make the incision and once the tumor was visible, they would continually check my blood levels via an arterial line to see what happened when they touched the area with a probe. If the numbers jumped, then it was likely parathyroid cancer, an extremely rare cancer that only accounts for 0.005 percent of all cancers. If that was the case, then they would remove the affected parathyroid gland and re-implant another, remove part of the thyroid and leave half to function, and give me a natural thyroid hormone. If the parathyroid did not appear to be malignant, then they would remove the gland with the tumor and perform a full thyroidectomy.

I've always wanted to be unique. I didn't quite mean 0.005 percent unique, but spoiler alert, Dr. DeJong's relentless studying of my chart would pay off.

Around 3 p.m. a surgical team poked their heads around the curtain of the pre-op room and told me it was time to head in. Up until this point, other than considering jumping out of the car, I had played it really cool even though I was a complete mess inside. I wanted to be home making dinner and sipping a glass of wine. This wasn't fair, but still, I played it cool. Until a big old-school nurse noticed that I hadn't taken off my engagement ring.

"Honey, you can't have that in surgery. You were told to take off *all* jewelry," she snarked.

That was all it took. A cascade of tears erupted as my voice caught while I was trying to say, "But I just got it," making me sound like I was six and trying to keep a puppy.

Let me tell you about my ring. It is a three-quarter carat princess cut set high in a white-gold band. It's simple. Out of everything in our lives together, this ring is the only thing that is simple. Terry told me he wanted to get me a bigger one a few months after he proposed, to which I emphatically responded no.

You see, this ring represents so much more than a piece of jewelry to me. It represents the impossible becoming possible. It represents what a diamond truly is. When tectonic plates collide, one enormous land mass is forced underneath the other into an area known as the subduction zone. If one of these plates carries rocks and material rich in carbon content, it melts under the high temperature and pressure to create diamonds. This is very much like our relationship.

We collided like tectonic plates, causing massive changes deep inside. We both felt the weight of being in that subduction zone as we navigated through divorce. We both carried traits and talents that were buried, much like the carbon content deep within the rocks. We were exposed to extreme pressure and heat while we were learning to love each other, and just like the diamond, when we emerged on the other side, we were crystal clear in our purest form and stronger than steel.

Diamonds are indestructible, and we believe that our relationship is too. Terry also had to work his fingers to the bone, literally working so hard that his hands would cramp in the morning, to keep our family floating. He worked hard and saved up a long time to be able to buy the ring. This ring represents all of that to me.

So keeping this ring on was like having a part of Terry with me during the scariest moment of my life. Having him hug a little part of me would surely make me feel a bit better. But none of that outweighed the precautions for surgery, and I had to slip the ring off of my finger and hand it to Terry to put in his pocket. All that was left to do now was to go to sleep. I felt like I had been stripped of everything. My clothes, my ring, my choices. A feeling that would continue for years.

"Okay, Jonelle, we are going to have you count backwards now, starting from ten."

I had been wheeled in and moved onto the surgical table. It was cold and sterile, and the smell of bleachy plastic burned my nose. I think it's funny how the surgical team moves around so quickly while you are lying perfectly still. So I counted, as asked, while the anesthesiologist placed a mask over my mouth and nose. "Ten, nine, eight, seven... I'm still awake... Six...and five..."

The next thing I remember is a crash and hectic commotion. Everything was black, and I was nauseated and confused. I couldn't see but I could hear, and people were yelling, "Whoa, whoa, whoa!" in panic-stricken voices. Someone was pushing me from a sitting to a lying position and holding their hand on my chest. It took all of my strength to open my eyes enough to see the blurry outline of a man in a lab coat inches from my face. I was even more confused, and as my eyes started to clear a bit, a wave of pain hit me like a punching bag. I started to cry, but I couldn't make noise. Someone was now inches away from my face with their hands on me to keep me down. As my eyes cleared even more, I began to focus on something familiar. It was Mickey Mouse.

As soon as I started to realize what was happening, I was knocked out and waking up again in a different room. This time other patients were in the room too, and I could hear a man yelling profanities and begging for help. It was like a thriller movie when they show someone going in and out of consciousness with a heartbeat audio track thumping in the background, the actor waking up to blurry sights, then passing back out only to wake up somewhere else, usually tied to a chair in a warehouse. But this was real, and it's exactly how I remember waking up from surgery seven hours later.

Finally, after what seemed like days, I began waking up for good. There is a vivid image in my head that brings peace to me when I visualize it. When I was stable enough to leave the recovery room, a transport aid pushed my bed down a few halls and into an elevator. When the elevator doors opened, we were in another hall of an indoor bridge that connected one tower to another. It was dimly lit and calming.

Suddenly the aid stopped pushing my bed, and in a South African accent, she softly said, "Look out there, dear. It's the lights." I lifted my heavy head and turned to the right to see a perfectly clear night sky packed full of stars, and poking up through the horizon was the Chicago skyline.

I love the Chicago skyline. When I was a little girl my parents would take us to Chicago and we would drive home at dusk, just as all of the lights in the skyscrapers would flip on. Like square stars, they seemed to magically appear. I would twist and contort my neck to look straight up at the Sears Tower and the Water Tower as we drove by. As we would travel south down Lake Shore Drive, I would count as many buildings as I could, in awe of their towering lights.

Once we exited on 55 South, I would turn around and watch out the back window as the skyline slowly became smaller and smaller until finally we were too far south to see it. I would tear up and feel a heavy tug of sadness in my chest once we were only surrounded by corn and bean fields again.

Even as a child the pulse of the city was something that I could feel and craved, so when I saw the skyline from my hospital bed, it was as if an old familiar friend greeted me and said, "Hey, everything will be okay now. You were lost for a few hours, but you know me like the back of your hand. Welcome home."

At the end of the hall, waiting for me to come up were my dad and Terry. Seeing my dad was the second event that helped me clear my foggy head and start to come back to the present. It was 11 p.m. and I had only been gone for eight hours, but it felt like I had been to Mars and back.

Terry and my mom stayed with me in the hospital, and the next morning I felt much better. So much better that I got up and put on makeup before the physicians even started their rounds. This was the first time I saw my incision. A three-inch long horizontal cut from left to right taped together with eight vertical Steri-Strips represented the seven-hour ordeal. The arterial line had left my whole left forearm black and blue. I felt a little like Frankenstein and looked like I had been in some sort of back alley fight.

Around 10 a.m., twelve hours after coming out of recovery, Dr. DeJong and a handful of surgical students appeared in the doorway. "There she is," a cheerful voice said. The students, however, didn't look quite as cheerful. They actually looked a little scared.

Dr. DeJong checked my surgical site and explained what they had done in surgery. The had removed the tumor and the borders were clear, and I was officially cancer free. He explained to me that I woke up a little earlier than they had anticipated once the procedure was over and sat straight up in the operating room, pulling my breathing tube and knocking over a metal tray full of tools. He said with a little chuckle that I really freaked out the students present in the OR. That explained the crash. That also explained the look on the students' faces.

Two days after being discharged I went to the local hospital to have some blood work done and levels checked. Terry was pulling the car around to park and was going to meet me inside. We had been home for a couple of days, and things seemed to be going well aside from being tired and a little sore. Once the blood work was done, I stood up to leave and the room started to spin. I felt like I couldn't breathe and my face felt tingly. I told the phlebotomist that I felt like I was going to pass out, so she sat me in a wheelchair and asked if I was feeling any better. I wasn't. Now I felt like I couldn't feel anything. Not my hands, my feet, my face…nothing.

She wheeled me down the hall to the emergency department and Terry joined us along the walk somewhere. They took me right to a trauma room, where my friend and the head nurse that day, Lisa, was waiting for me. Lisa is steady and calm all the time. Not much gets her worked up, and she was cool as a cucumber as she took my vitals and watched my face, trying to assess the situation.

"I think I'm having a stroke. Am I having a stroke, Lisa? What's happening? Is it a stroke?" I repeated over and over.

Not taking her eyes off of me, she calmly said, "I don't think so." Just then the emergency room doctor appeared, and I heard Lisa say, "I think she's having a panic attack."

And that is when I realized that everything had changed.

I can't explain how. I have never been able to explain how, but something during those seven hours changed me. For a few years I felt like my face looked different. Almost like I didn't recognize parts of it. I thought maybe I had actually had a stroke that was missed, but between Terry and my medical team, I was reassured that I looked exactly the same. I physically felt different, too, in ways I can't explain, but I also started having heart palpitations that would stop me in my tracks and make me stand frozen with my finger on my neck, counting out heartbeats and panicking when I felt the skip or pound of a premature ventricular contraction.

But the biggest change was my constant state of anxiety. Panic attacks became a daily event. We tried essential oils, we tried soft music, we tried breathing exercises. We bought candles, bath oil, heated sheets. We even got a dog. Nothing worked. I was panicked because I felt different. I think I felt different because I was panicking. It was a terrible cycle. I knew that music was healing, so I counted down the weeks until I was released to sing again.

Finally after a long six weeks, Dr. DeJong released me from any restrictions, and it was time. I could go back to my job, my love, my healer. But when Terry pulled out the guitar to warm me up, I opened my mouth and a scratchy squeak was all I was able to produce. It felt as if someone was taking their hand and squeezing my neck, choking me and cutting off the air necessary to sing. We tried a few more times and thought that maybe I just needed a little more rest, but as the weeks went on, I still couldn't sing, so we made an appointment at Loyola with Dr. DeJong to see if he could figure out what was happening.

The report was good. Kind of. Everything from a physical standpoint checked out. I was reassured that during surgery, none of the alarms that are triggered when a vocal cord nerve is in danger went off, but I still couldn't sing. I was referred to a throat specialist who put a camera down my throat to observe my vocal cords. Good news was that everything looked intact and the vocal cords themselves were moving the way they should. The bad news was that the vocal cord nerve was a bit stunned, which could either get better on its own or stay that way for life. There was no way of telling and no way to improve it. It was all up to my body and God.

Anger is an emotion that comes in a disguise. Sometimes the disguise is so good that you can even trick yourself into believing that what you're feeling is not actually anger. That only lasts until you finally pull off the mask and unveil the seething, boiling fury that eventually bubbles over, leaving you in a heap on the floor, empty of tears, empty of emotion, and numb. This roller-coaster can be relentless, taking you on its upward climb of hope only to drop you down a twisting and turning dark tunnel, free falling with no bottom to hit. Just when you think you're done for, the light peeks through the cracks, and you climb out of the darkness again.

This is the best way I can describe my next year.

Peeps, I was *angry*. Not just a little upset but flat out angry. I felt different and I wanted my "old" self back. I looked different, and everywhere I went I could feel people staring at my throat. I imagined they must have been wondering if I had been attacked. I wanted to hiss at them, "Yes, as a matter of fact, I was attacked. By an ugly, evil thief named cancer who stole my voice."

I laid in bed and cried. I ate. I gained weight and ate more. I stayed home and felt sorry for myself while the band played. I called Terry's phone over and over on nights when he was playing and I was at home, and I would pick a fight when he didn't answer...even though he was playing and I knew it.

I got dressed and decided to go watch the band play but at the last minute changed my mind and put sweats back on and stayed home. I put makeup on and came to shows pretending to enjoy some drinks until the last set, when I had downed a six-pack of mini Rieslings and marched out the front door and down the middle of Washington Street. When one of the guys suggested I drink a bottle of water, I cleared a table full of empty beer bottles and watched as they crashed to the floor, shattering into tiny shards, and flipped off the people who were startled and staring at me in disbelief. I was grounded to the car when I wanted to try to sing on stage after a martinis-on-an-empty-stomach night. Terry, trying to protect me, wouldn't let me near the stage, and I screamed in front of a whole swanky restaurant, "What, are you EMBARRASSED by me?!"

Ugh. Even typing this is making me cringe, but it's the truth and I am not about to sit here and tell you that I handled that year gracefully and elegantly. Nope. I handled it by drinking cheap wine and crying on my dog.

I had started working with a voice coach in the city to see if I could possibly rehab my way back to the stage. We were working toward a goal and had made a tiny bit of progress. For one particular session, my parents had driven me to Chicago and took me to dinner afterwards. The band was playing at Clayton's, and my parents dropped me off once we got back to town. I walked in the front door and it was wall-to-wall jammed, loud, and brightly lit. I immediately regretted my decision, but it was too late—my parents were long gone.

I made my way to the back room, pushing through groups of people who were laughing and talking. My head felt wooshy from the change of atmosphere; going from a nice warm, quiet car ride to a party scene was a bit overstimulating. On my journey to the back room, people stopped me to ask how I was. There was a lot of love being shown to me at this time, but my anger had total control over me. So I was annoyed. It didn't help that along with not being able to sing, I was unable to yell or speak loudly, so it was hard to have a conversation over the noise, and when I did try to speak louder I couldn't project or hear myself, so it caused me a great deal of anxiety.

When I finally made it to the back room, I took a half of a deep breath when Terry saw me and winked at me, and before I could get the rest of the breath in I heard him say on the mic, "Jonelle, come on up here and sing one, honey. Let's get her up here." What in the actual hell was happening? Why would he do this to me? Why would he call me on the stage to sing? I wasn't ready.

I could barely get a note out, but everyone was cheering so loudly, and I think someone may have actually picked me up and set me on the stage. The next thing I knew, I had a microphone in my hand and the band started playing "I'm Yours" by Jason Mraz. I squealed and stuttered my way through the song. It was a train wreck—I knew it and the crowd knew it and the band knew it…but the show must go on. So they continued to play and I continued to squeak, and finally after a torturous three minutes, it was over.

I took two steps toward the stage stairs and just like in the hospital lab, everything started to get numb. I grabbed our friend Jason, another musician who happened to be out that night, and told him that I felt like I was going to pass out. The sound of the band, the clinking of the bottles, the cheering of the crowd all faded away to a loud ringing in my ears.

Jason threw me in the car and drove me to the hospital. Another panic attack. I was at the point where I couldn't imagine my life without panic. This was my new reality. Somewhere on that surgical table was my old self, and I was determined to get her back. Another spoiler alert…I never did. And I am so happy that I didn't.

It took me over a year to sing again, and I'm still learning how to handle panic and anxiety. To my anxiety sisters and brothers, I know it feels like you're being swallowed whole, trapped in the mouth of a monster. I know that something as small as a change in the weather or a time change can throw off your whole game. I understand how it feels to *know* that you're outgoing and expressive but suddenly feel like an introvert who doesn't want to have to communicate with other people. It can be confusing, and it can make you feel like something is wrong with you. It can feel like the bad is never going to end. Like you are a record that is skipping and no one, no amount of sleep, no amount of food, no amount of love can lift the needle. I understand.

Please hear me. It will get better.

Be gentle with yourself. If you need to take a month or two months or a year or longer to get right with yourself, then do it. You owe no one any explanation. If you need to drink peppermint tea and soak in a warm bath full of Epsom salts and lavender oil, then by all means, soak away. But I want to ask you to do one thing for me: be good to your body.

Fill yourself with healthy proteins and fruits and vegetables and a ton of water with lemon. Move your body. You don't have to do CrossFit (but if you want to do CrossFit, then go right ahead), just move in some way. Take a walk around the park. Breathe in the air and feel it in your lungs and slowly breathe out, knowing that you have purpose and strength. Turn on some old-school rap and dance in your kitchen until your cheeks are rosy and your arms are sore from waving them around like you just don't care. Do something to get moving.

And for God's sake, please sleep. Get yourself on a sleep schedule and listen to the Ocean Waves station on Pandora while you fall asleep. Get a sweater blanket and a good pillow with a cool, crisp pillowcase and make your bed a sanctuary. Buy yourself a teddy bear. Yep, you heard me. Something to hold on to. Set your alarm to wake you up early in the morning, pour yourself a cup of tea, and start again… and this last one is the big one….

If you feel like you are past the point of baths and tea and sleep, please don't feel ashamed to talk to someone professionally, and if you need help now, call someone. Tell them.

Remember that you are loved and needed, and you are bigger and more important than this monster that has you in its grip.

Chapter 10
Freedom Of Love

Picture this. I'm at a birthday party full of six-year-olds at a nail spa, and I'm chatting away with Jodie, the stylist who does my hair, while waiting for our little girls' pink piggies to dry. "The owner is selling the salon," she says in a worried tone. "You should buy it," she jokes, and we laugh and say our goodbyes, our little blondies pulling at our hands.

I had just started learning to sing again and was still working at the hospital, but health care had changed for me once I came back from medical leave. Every time I smelled that "hospital smell", I felt like I was back in the recovery room. I knew I was having some post-traumatic stress, but I didn't want to allow myself that label. I was experiencing extreme survivor's guilt, something no one told me about, nor is it talked about much. I felt like I wasn't worthy of having PTSD. I hadn't been through a war or a death and I didn't undergo chemo or radiation. I didn't lose my hair or have to try to live with the debilitating pain that can come with treatment. I was cancer free. So what if I couldn't sing? How selfish of me to feel sorry for myself.

So I pushed down these feelings and slapped myself in the face with a "don't you dare act like you have been through hell" attitude. Except that I wasn't okay, and every time someone got bad news in the clinic or was transferred by ambulance due to the severity of their illness or injury, I felt it well up in my throat.

The final straw came when a young patient came in and went into cardiac arrest. The doctor on duty, one of my good friends, called out an order to get the automated external defibrillator (AED), so I ran and grabbed it off of the wall. He told me to get the paddles ready, but instead of moving fast like I had been trained to do, I stood frozen holding the paddles up in each hand.

"Jonelle I need the AED *now*!" he shouted and finally grabbed them out of my hands.

I was trembling, and when the ambulance finally left with the patient, I sat at the break room table with my head in my hands. The doctor knocked on the frame of the open door and asked if he could join me. He reassured me that it was okay. That the first time he dealt with his first cardiac arrest, he felt the same way. But I knew that it was time for me to go.

I kept replaying the conversation I had with Jodie. I knew that it wasn't possible to buy a salon. We were already living paycheck to paycheck, and my credit wasn't in the best condition since I was still recovering financially from the divorce.

I kept the conversation to myself for three days before I

finally told Terry about it. At first I laughed a little snort as if to say, "Yeah right, can you believe that someone actually thinks I could buy a business and run it?"

But when I said it out loud again to Lois, she replied with, "Why not?" I gave her a list of at least ten reasons "why not" and Lois, being the brilliant businesswoman she is, shot back with ten reasons why my reasons were invalid. Two days later she had set up a meeting for us with a local bank vice president. A week later I called the owner to find out how much she was looking to sell for, and on May 1, 2012 we bought Roots Hair Studio.

Ten days later, in an ultra private ceremony consisting of Terry, me, our friend Jason, and our dear friend and judge, Lance, we said our vows while standing face to face on a wooden bridge covering the Illinois & Michigan Canal. We thought long and hard about what kind of wedding we wanted. We both had large weddings previously and didn't feel pulled toward that experience again. We also couldn't figure out a date that worked for all our kids to be present, and we wouldn't leave any of them out. But the biggest deciding factor for having a private ceremony was that we spend most days of our lives surrounded by people. It's not that we don't love our people. We do. We love our people fiercely. It's just that we live a very public life and make almost all of our memories accessible via our public social media pages, and we wanted to keep this one to ourselves. So on May 11, 2012, I became Mrs. Terry Carter and the song of my life began.

When you start to manifest an intention it becomes a reality. Read that again. We talked about it earlier, but here I was once again setting intentions and manifesting them by putting things into action. Is it scary? You bet it is. Is it exciting? More than you can imagine. It's also hard work, and the ability to be open-minded enough to keep learning. If you think you know it all, you don't.

It took me a long time to figure out how to run a business and put the right key players in place to make it successful. I still don't know it all and continue to learn every day. I have made big mistakes and lost money, but I stay true to who I am and run my business the way that I run my home—with love, respect, and detail. I go the extra mile and try my best to make it feel like home.

Some of my ideas have failed. Once I decided that I wanted to bake gourmet cupcakes. I made a list of over 100 flavors, bought pounds of flour and sugar, and whipped up three dozen cupcakes: double chocolate, Key lime, and Horchata. I brought some to my neighbors and some to work. Orders flew in, but there was a little glitch. I hated making cupcakes, and I was awful at frosting them. I mean, a five-year-old would have frosted them better. I actually told everyone that Marley decorated her four-year-old birthday cake, but the truth was that I did it.

I tried to launch a program recognizing women, called the Hard-Working Women's Award. The idea was that the salon girls would pick a hard-working woman in our community and surprise her at home or work with flowers, balloons, a framed award, and a gift certificate for a free service at the salon. It never stuck, and after three or four months it was forgotten. I actually asked Terry while writing this what we called that program because I couldn't remember.

These are just a couple of the ideas I've had that made

it off paper. My point is, not everything you try will work. Not every idea will make it off the paper and even if it does, that doesn't mean it's for you. Then one day, something clicks. It works and you realize that all of the hard work, all of the trial and error, the second-guessing, the feeling like a failure, was worth it.

Nine months after buying the salon and using what we had left of our loan to remodel, I got a call from Heather at six thirty in the morning.

"I think the apartments above the salon are on fire," she said in a half-yell, half-calm voice.

I shot out of bed and immediately pressed the button to turn on the scanner app I had downloaded on my phone (yes, I have the tendency to be nosy). The second the scanner app opened I heard a man with a deep, concerned voice say, "Roots Hair Studio. Can someone get a hold of the owner?"

The salon was on fire.

I think we have to try to see the positive in any situation. I truly believe that down in my bones, but as much as I am an optimistic dreamer, there are days when I have to fight to stay on top. There are days when I want to chuck it all in and say screw it. This day and the following days were "chuck it in" days. I was fighting to sing. I had quit my day job. They always say not to do that…but I did. I had borrowed money from the bank and sank every penny into a business that was struggling from day one. The previous owner didn't tell her clientele that someone was taking over the business, so everyone thought she had closed down, which made it even trickier to build up. And now the place burned down.

Here is where it is extra important to pay attention. I could drop an inspirational quote right about now that says something about winners never quitting, but let's get real for a second. Winners know when to pause and when to keep going. Winners know how to take a loss and learn from it. Winners know that winning doesn't come free or easily.

So two days after the fire, my team and I stood among the ashes and, covered in soot, we sorted through melted plastic perm rods and pieces of furniture that were blackened and broken. And believe me when I tell you that we had moments when we did quit. There were days I when I would walk into the cold, dark salon (since it still lacked power), take one look at the ruins, and turn right back around to leave.

What makes this a winning situation is that eventually I went back. In the midst of chaos, it's unrealistic to think that you won't have a moment that makes you stop for a second. Winning doesn't mean exhausting yourself to the point of failure because you have been taught that "winners never quit", but what it does mean is that you finish—even if you have to pause—gracefully.

Let's compare this theory to working out. Ro, my trainer, has taught me that even if I have a day or a week when I fall off the wagon and eat pie for breakfast, lunch, and dinner, or if I don't do as many squats as the day before, it doesn't mean I've lost. If I need to pause, it's okay. It's okay to quit—for a moment. What makes you successful is being able to continue.

It took nine months for the salon's reconstruction to be completed. Out of the ashes came a beautiful new space that continues to grow and flourish. Our salon family is made up of talented and experienced professionals savvy in the cutting-edge beauty industry, but more than that, we are a team of women who love other women and want to help them rise up. We have created a space where it is safe to think outside the box. A space where being your authentic self is encouraged and supported. A space that brings peace and calm not only to our guests but to each other.

I started a private label skin care and cosmetics company called "J.Carter Skin Care & Cosmetics", not just another dream of mine but also another avenue to helping women look and feel their best. I am beyond proud of what Roots has evolved into, and it has been exciting watching this very special team of artistic businesswomen continue to grow. Whenever I am unsure how to handle a situation, I think back to my JCP days with Kelly Brown and try to move forward with grace.

Things started to seem like they were looking up a little after the fire. I felt like I could finally focus on starting to move forward with my new self, but there were a few things left that I still needed to do.

A year or so before I got sick, I ran into Ed. Remember a while back when I said that I had one more encounter and two more phone conversations with him? Here is the rest of that story.

When Ed was in high school, he worked for a shop in the town next to us. Once he started to become fairly well known, he would come back once a year and hold a seminar at the shop's open house. After we lost contact I forgot about the open house every single year until I would drive by and see all the cars parked at the shop. Every year it hit me like a bolt of lightning as I unassumingly drove to the grocery store or the post office and turned the corner to see that Ed was in town. This was a special kind of hurt. You see, it used to be that seeing me was the highlight of his trip home, and now he didn't even bother to let me know he was back.

So as you can imagine, my heart started pounding on this particular chilly spring day when I was heading to get gas and saw a parking lot full of cars. I called Terry, who was at work, and told him that Ed was in town, to which he replied, "Go get your closure, sweetheart."

You're probably wondering why the hell I would tell my husband anything about my emotions toward Ed. I mean, shouldn't he be threatened or jealous? No, for two reasons.

The first reason is that Terry isn't a jealous guy. He doesn't feel threatened by anyone because he knows where I stand and he knows where our relationship is. Our divorces were like a living nightmare and we went through that together. A bond like that isn't easily broken. The second reason is that we are both empathetic humans. We have an innate ability to understand and share the feelings of others. We are able to easily and completely put ourselves in another person's shoes. Because of this, it's easy to understand that just because we might have unfinished business or emotions about a situation does not mean that we're in any way trying to hurt each other.

Friends, this way of thinking does not come easily, but it comes with time, patience, and trust. Terry understood my need to have an uncomfortable conversation in order to gain closure, so with his blessing I walked into the store where Ed was giving his seminar.

I had planned this moment in my head for a long time, mulling over the details and rehearsing what I would say if I had the opportunity. I wanted him to know that the girl he saw the last time we were together was lost, hurt, and scared. I wanted to tell him how much I had grown and learned since then and that I was brave and strong and had finally gained some self-respect. I wanted to tell him that I could finally see myself as the person that he saw me as when we were younger. I wanted to forgive him for hurting me, hold my head high, walk out with closure and a mended spirit, go home, tip a glass of champagne in honor of our years of friendship, and move on. But when I walked in and saw him standing in the back of the store just finishing up a presentation, I froze. I was frozen solid, and it only got worse from there.

Remember when I warned you about the cringeworthy night with Sam? Well, ladies and gentleman, hold on to your hats because what you are about to see has not been attempted by anyone to date, or at least anyone sane... okay, maybe it's been attempted. But this...*this* has to be the most awkward thing to admit. *Sigh*. Here it goes.

I walked in and asked the greeter if Ed was presenting, and he pointed me in the direction of where he was speaking. My body walked toward the back, but my adrenaline was rushing so fast that it actually felt like I was floating. Ed was now signing autographs and taking pictures with each attendee, and as I approached the presentation area, he looked up and our eyes locked. A piercing hot wave of acid rose up in my chest and forced me to clench my jaw hard. I kept walking and I would have walked right up to him, but I was stopped by a woman who said, "Ma'am, the line starts back here."

Damn. Now what? He already saw me. He looked nervous. I couldn't just turn around and walk out, although looking back, I wish I had.

So I sheepishly got in line and watched as one by one, fans made small talk and took pictures and swooned over his newfound fame. One by one his fans excitedly fluttered away, and one by one I was closer to being the next fan in line. This moment was humiliating for me. I closed my eyes and drew in a breath through my nose, hoping that maybe I would open my eyes and be somewhere else. Anywhere else. But I was stuck in line, and when the person in front of me stepped away, there was nothing left between us but a few feet and awkwardness.

"Jonelle," he said in a tone that sounded as if he'd forced my name out of his mouth. We exchanged a weird half-hug, and he kept looking over my shoulder and around to see who was watching. I don't know which one of us wanted to melt into the floor more. "How are you?" he asked, and this is when everything went to hell.

Instead of just saying, "Fine, I'm fine, but I came here to say goodbye," I started spewing out lie after lie, and not just little white lies…*big* lies. Big, huge, fake lies. As I write this, I am closing my eyes and breathing through my nose right now just to get through this part of the book.

I told him that I had been signed to a record label and was about to go on tour. Yep, I said that. You are closing your eyes now too, aren't you? I told him that I had never been happier and that I was just stopping in to say hi. And then after three minutes of fake smiling (both of us) and uncomfortable silences filled with more of my lies, he told me he had to go. So I gave him a peace sign (whyyyyyy a peace sign? Ugh.) and he told me to tell my parents hello, and that was it. I turned around and walked out the door.

I wasn't even halfway to my car when my back molar crumbled in my mouth, and an hour later I was lying in the dentist's chair for an emergency dental appointment. I cried all the way home. Post-dental drooling, crying, coughing. It was quite a dramatic scene.

By the time I got home, it was getting dark out and Terry was home waiting for me with warm arms. I fell into his arms like I had done so many times in the past and would do again many times in the future, and just like that everything was okay again.

The first phone call came a few months after surgery. Around this time I was still healing. Not so much physically but emotionally, and I had been reflecting a bunch and trying to heal myself completely. I thought that if I healed all of the wounds in my heart, maybe I would be able to sing again, and if I could sing again, maybe I would feel normal again. One of the jagged gaping wounds I was trying to close was the one left by Ed. So I got up my nerve and sent him an email that read as follows:

Hi Ed,
I hope you and your family are well. I need to talk to you. If you could give me a call sometime, I would appreciate it.
Take Care,
Jonelle

I left him my work number and hit send. A few hours later he called. Once again, I was instantly awkward, and even though I had the floor, I was just not sure how to start. So I told him I had been diagnosed with cancer but was better and I just wanted him to know. But more than that, I needed to know what happened with us.

At first he acted like he didn't know what I was talking about, until he finally did, and then he just kept saying that he didn't mean to hurt me but he was only trying to get me to do what he would want his wife to do. He said he still thought the world of me.

We agreed it would be okay to have a small amount of contact and said we would be better about staying in touch. It all felt very forced and fast, but I was happy. I felt like I had a little part of the old me back, and at this time in my life that was everything.

The second phone call would come about a year later. This would be the very last time I would have any contact with Ed to date. It had been a while since we'd exchanged a text or email, something that only occurred twice in the year since we were slightly reunited.

I heard a song while cleaning the house that made me think of him. Don't get any ideas. I'm a musician, and music represents everything to me and makes me think of friends just as much as it makes me think of lovers. I shot off a quick text that said, "Hey! Been a while. Just saying hi. Hope you and your family are well," and went back to cleaning. Within fifteen minutes my phone rang and it was Ed. I will save you all of the boring mundane details and get to the gory part. He said that he didn't think we should have any contact anymore, and then he dropped the bomb on me. He said, "You make me uncomfortable."

Wowza. That one hurt. More than some words might.

I told him that I understood and we both said to "take care" and that was all she wrote. That ongoing song in my world finally came to an end. Sometimes I peek in on social media to see what he's up to and make sure he's doing well. Sometimes when I least expect it, his picture or a video shows up in my world and makes me sad for a while. There have been a few times while going through trials when I have thought about reaching out, but then I remember that I gave him my word, and I will not go back on it.

I have tried to understand the lessons I'm supposed to learn from this experience. I'm not sure I comprehend them yet, but I do know that I frequently pull from these emotions and write songs. "The Pitcher" is about him. So is "Tequila and Whiskey". Now when you listen to those songs, you might have a different view of them. Maybe they will help you learn some lessons too.

It took me another year or so to really start to feel safe singing again. We had been writing like crazy and had been playing with River Road as much as we possibly could. We were starting to build a nice following and had booked the Nebraska State Fair.

This was a special trip for me that not only put us on a big stage and in front of news cameras, but it also put a piece of my heart back in place. A big radio station in Grand Island had agreed to have us on their morning show, Franzman's *One Man Party in the Morning*. Franzman is one of the best radio personalities in the country. He was also the best man at Charlie and my wedding.

Steve Franzman was born and raised on the East Coast and was Charlie's roommate in the early 2000s. When Charlie moved to Illinois, Steve came to live near us. When Steve and I first met, we had a bit of a power struggle over wanting Charlie's attention. I wanted all of Charlie's time because he'd just moved to Illinois and we had never experienced life together yet, and Steve wanted Charlie's time because he knew absolutely no one in Illinois.

Right from the start, Steve and I were like siblings, but not in the "dream world" way of saying "Oh em gee, we're like sister and brother!" Oh no, it was much more "Oh em gee, we're like a sister and brother who can't stand each other." For the first few weeks we exchanged snarky comments and eye rolls and loud sighs. I bitched about him. He bitched about me. Until one day all three of us ended up in a car on a road trip to Connecticut. We weren't even halfway through Indiana when I had a complete meltdown.

Have you ever seen *Shrek 2*? When Donkey is in the back of the carriage and keeps asking Shrek over and over if they're there yet? This was the scene. We had stopped for lunch and were having tacos at a picnic table rest area. Steve, in true brother fashion, was picking on me relentlessly. I finally had enough and lost my temper. I stood up fast and slammed my taco down on the ground so hard that lettuce and meat flew everywhere, but that wasn't enough. I started stomping on it and stomping hard. I was taking all of the aggression from the last few weeks out on the crunchy shell. I swore at it and yelled at it and finally after it was completely pulverized, I stood silently, instantly regretting destroying my lunch.

Steve was staring at me in disbelief when he suddenly

broke out in uncontrolled laughter, which then made me start to laugh, until we were both laughing so hard that we were crying. It's hard to explain, but after that moment we had an unbreakable bond. We did everything together like the three musketeers, and when Charlie and I got married, Steve stood up as our best man. He had announced only days before that he landed a radio job in Joplin, Missouri and would be moving in a few short weeks. Steve had gone to broadcasting school during his time in Chicago and was really good at it. I was proud of him for finding his first radio job but deeply saddened by his relocation.

Our bond came to a screeching halt when he found out that Charlie and I were getting divorced. He was so angry with me and me with him. I felt like he had no idea what I had been going through that led up to something as serious as divorce, and he felt like the two people who made love seem attainable were letting him down. Quite frankly, that scared the shit out of him. So we stopped talking. We even blocked each other on social media and eliminated each other completely from our lives.

It wasn't until I reached out a few years later that we started to mend our friendship in the most beautiful way. I was in a rough spot with Charlie. He had been having trouble getting back into the workforce after losing his job and things were looking really bad for him. I was worried about him. Even though he was my ex-husband, I felt a responsibility to at least check on his well-being. He had no family and few friends here, and he was, after all, my daughter's father and someone that I had shared a life with.

After a semi-intervention (i.e., me sitting in his disheveled apartment eating a hot pizza that I brought and begging him to get himself some help) I sent Steve a Facebook message asking him if I could please talk to him about something important. He called me later that day and we talked for over an hour. He had been having conversations with Charlie that were frustrating and not going anywhere. He had basically stepped into my role that I played while married to Charlie and finally understood why I had to make a change. He understood why I filed for divorce because he was basically divorcing Charlie too.

We cried and apologized over and over and caught up with each other. Steve was doing great in Nebraska and told me about his career and I told him all about Terry, a guy he hated before even knowing him just a few short years before. We decided that we needed to see each other, and the Nebraska State Fair seemed like the best possibility. So the band applied and scored a slot on the Bristol Windows Stage for that upcoming August. Kyle, Terry, and I set off on our first out-of-state road trip as a band.

A few weeks prior we had held an album fundraising concert and had raised enough money to start the process of recording our first album, so we had a lot to discuss as we made our way through the rolling hills of western Iowa and into Nebraska. Meanwhile, Charlie had finally given up on Illinois and moved back east, where he still lives today. He left when Marley was just nine years old, but they have a unique and loving long-distance relationship. All too similar to the way we began. Full circle is an interesting term. This is what his move felt like for me.

Steve and Terry hit it off within minutes and Steve and I went right back to where we left off. It was so healing to have mended a friendship that was lost and had once been so important. This, as you can imagine, was incredibly important to me.

We had a great trip to Nebraska with a live performance on the radio, an NBC news interview, and another interview that night on Fox. Even though a tornado warning was issued while we were on stage, we still had a great time playing music for the people of Nebraska.

Sometimes it's easy to forget how things can change so drastically and quickly in life. One minute you're trying to figure out how to fill up your gas tank and the next you're holding a winning lottery ticket. One day you're having a conversation with your sweet grandma and the next day she's gone. One season of your life you are so close to a friend that you're practically family, the next season you are strangers, and yet the next season you are being interviewed on their morning show hundreds of miles away from where you met in the first place. Nothing, nothing, nothing stays the same. We are on a planet that is spinning and rotating and in constant movement. We are not meant to be stagnant.

I think this can work positively in our lives if we choose to think of it that way. Meaning, live each day knowing that things can change fast. If things are beautiful and good in your world, soak it all in with thankfulness. Don't waste time worrying about things that don't matter. Don't live in fear but live fully in gratitude. If things are dark and feel hopeless, try to remember that everything shifts and transitions, and the darkness *will* be replaced by light. It will not stay dark forever. If we live our lives respecting the knowledge that things will change, we can live out our lives with no regrets and plenty of hope.

On our trip home we booked studio time in Bloomington, Illinois with a producer Kyle had worked with in the past. Erik Nelson would end up becoming the brains and talent behind our first album, multiple singles including our first single to hit the radio, and would play live with us for special shows like our appearance on Chicago's own *WGN Morning News*. I give Erik and his gifted mind, originality, and innovative thinking the credit of making our first album everything that we imagined it could be and more.

We had a handful of sad country songs and plenty of happier songs written. Terry and I had just finished a trip to Lake Geneva, Wisconsin, where we booked an off-season room at the old Playboy Mansion and had full intentions of doing absolutely nothing at all. Week after week we had been playing music three to four times a week, and we needed a break. The morning we were leaving for vacation, Terry announced that he wasn't going to take a guitar because we just needed to get away, but that was a fleeting thought. At the last minute, we pulled back into the driveway and threw a guitar in the car and headed north. Seven hours later, after an hours-long drive and dinner, we were sitting in our hotel room staring at each other when the tug-of-war of this conversation began.

"What do *you* want to do?"

"I don't care. What do you want to do?"

"Just tell me. I'm up for anything."

"Me too…you tell me."

I finally decided to take a bath and Terry decided to pull out the guitar while he waited for me. I could hear him strumming and singing something while I soaked in the sweet lavender bubble bath. When I emerged from the bath and rejoined Terry in our room, he told me to sit and listen for a second. He had a second chorus for "The One You Need", and before we knew it we were jotting down lyrics and singing into my phone's voice recorder.

Hours ticked by and I don't even think I had taken my towel off of my head when we finished the last line. It was one of those moments when silence spoke volumes. It felt as if a door had closed and another opened. Like some closure from the beginning of the cancer diagnosis had finally occurred.

A few years later, this song would become the theme song for a young mom who was losing her sight and hearing. A young woman who has become a sweet friend. This is a perfect example of why we are all meant to use our gifts. We *have* to live our purpose. Humanity needs us to use our gifts and talents to help each other through life. If we all harvested wheat but no one understood the art of baking, we would never have bread. Sorry, gluten-free peeps. It was the first thing that came to mind, but you get the point.

This is how I feel about all of the songs on the *Unloaded* album and all of the singles that have followed. Like I have been entrusted with a message and that I am simply a vessel. This is how I feel about this book, too, and the blog and all our social media posts and all my public speaking. All of these are ways I can share a message that someone might need to hear. So even though we haven't been nominated for any kind of Grammy or CMA, we still feel like we are winning every time someone approaches us and tells us how our music has touched them. Like the job we've been given is done.

Let's talk about our songs for a minute. The *Unloaded* album came together fairly quickly once we compiled all of our songs. "Lucky" was the first song on the album followed by "Bar Room Walls", a gritty classic country song about a dude who spends his time in a local tavern and thinks he's a Casanova, but at the end of the night he goes home with a six-pack of beer and a deflated ego.

Next up is "Unloaded", the album's title track. "Unloaded" came from a conversation that I had with a woman who was fed up with her life after her husband left her with the kids, a minivan payment, and a deep ache to feel sexy and strong again. "Unloaded" took us a few years to write because Terry and I couldn't agree on a chord progression. He was hearing something totally different than I was, and we would sit down to hash it out and finally give up after a few hours. It wasn't until we were in the studio working when Erik played it on the piano and it all came together. Although it is one of my favorite songs, it didn't gain as much popularity as "Lucky" or our singles to come.

Then came "Angel Eyes" (Art's song) and "The Pitcher" (Ed's song). Just like "The One You Need", "The Pitcher" came to me in the shower. There's something about me and water, I guess. It was late after a show and I was feeling a little defeated. Ed's memory had snuck in, uninvited, as it would so often do, and urged me to just peek at his public social media page. This is never a good road. It goes something like this. I type his name into the search bar (I still have enough pride to not follow any of his pages), click on his name, scroll down, and see a post about his latest win. I read about how much money it made him (millions now) and how all of his dreams came true. Enter pit in stomach. I have learned over the years to use the pit to write songs.

So here I am, in the shower thinking about how we grew up in such a small town that there must only be room for one success story and it's Ed's. Not mine. And so "The Pitcher" was born. After "The Pitcher", a song called "Anymore" begins. "Anymore" is one of our favorite songs and one that wasn't written until well into our time at the recording studio. If you have attended a live River Road show, then there's a good chance you've heard this story.

While driving home from a show late one night, Terry and I were having a bit of a heated discussion about our marriage. It began when one of us said something about the other not doing certain things anymore like, "You never kiss my cheek anymore," followed by, "Well *you* never give me a chance anymore," and on and on until we arrived home. Once in the house Terry went straight to bed, which added to my already red-hot face and frustration, so I went into our office and grabbed a guitar. I strummed a few chords and began writing about all of the things we fought about in the car.

Things were going exceptionally well until I ran out of chords I knew how to play and had to go wake up Terry to finish writing the song. It was such a good tune that we called Erik and told him that we had one more song to add to our album, and "Anymore" would go on to become one of our most downloaded tunes. "The One You Need" would come next, and finally the album was rounded out with a light-hearted, dreamy ragtime song called "Live Forever" that was born to be in a commercial or movie.

A little while after we released *Unloaded* I took a shot

in the dark and sent our single "Lucky" in an email to the drive-time afternoon guy at 98.3 WCCQ. WCCQ is one of the top country radio stations in our area. I have been listening to WCCQ since I was a kid. I used to call in on the all-request line and request songs. Bossman runs the show on weekday afternoons. He is a to-the-point, blunt but passionate radio personality, and I was surprised (and on the treadmill) when he replied right back and asked if it would be okay to spin it that night. It's a miracle I didn't fall off the treadmill when I read his response. Radio play is like gold to independent artists like us. Radio play during drive time on the best country radio station in the southwest suburbs is like a freaking diamond.

We would continue with this pattern from here on out. We write songs, fall in love with them, record them, fall in love even harder, release them, find an outlet (news, radio, live shows, live social media feeds) to push them out into the world and watch them grow.

Terry and I don't have any children of our own. We have songs. Those are our babies. We raise them up as best we can and put them out into the world with the hope that they will do well and touch lives and bring good into the universe. Just as we do when we raise our children. They are literally our babies.

As my songwriting grew, I continued to as well. I knew that I had a lot to say and that I wanted to use my voice to do more than sing. I truly felt it was time to be completely transparent about my journey thus far, so I began to think of ways I could do that. Public speaking was something I had always been interested in but didn't know how to start. Ask me to write you a song and I can take you from start to finish, but ask me to start a career in public speaking and you might as well ask me to start a career in cattle farming.

Still, like the stubborn dreamer I am, I threw it out into the universe.

Five whole years later I would get my opportunity as a keynote speaker in Ohio for a group of women at a professional development seminar. It came out of the blue after the founder heard a random show in the middle of nowhere that we were playing. This brings me to two pieces of solid advice. First, the universe doesn't know time like we do. Ever hear of God's speed? It can take days, months, years, or decades for something to solidify. Don't give up. If you put it out there and it's right for you, it will be. Not on your time (stop being so impatient) but in God's time.

Second—and this is a big one—if you are going to do something that you love, you *must* do it with every ounce of passion. Every. Single. Time.

No half-ass-ies. No holding back and saving it for another time, a bigger opportunity, etc. Nope. You must give it your all, all of the time, and you must do this for a couple of reasons. First off, you never ever know who's watching you. The big boss comes in many shapes, colors, and flavors, friends.

Once at a Phil Vasser concert that Heather and I were attending, a sad-looking middle-aged man sat alone behind us in the theater. Once in a while he would lean forward and ask us things like if we were enjoying the show, where we were from, and if we were big Phil fans. We were nice, if not a bit annoyed, but smiled and answered his questions between giving each other those sideways glances that girlfriends often do when they want to say "weeeiirdo" without actually saying it. I was, after all, too busy searching for someone with a backstage pass lanyard around their neck to possibly get backstage to bother with this guy who just wanted to chat us up.

When the show ended and the lights came up, we all stood and the man behind us tapped me on the shoulder. He handed us both a backstage pass. Extending his hand, he said, "Glad you liked the show, girls, I'm Phil's manager and I'll pass it along to him. Go on back and meet him."

I learned my lesson then and there. You do not know who someone is or who is watching you. It could be your big break, and if you don't show up, be kind to *everyone*, and treat everyone as if they are someone, then you might really screw up your chances.

So here we were in the middle of rural Illinois playing to a group of nine or ten people when this spunky woman approached me on break and asked to buy an album.

I happily obliged and we chatted for a few moments.

A week later she and I had a phone conversation, and she invited me to be the 2019 keynote speaker for The Power Of Her.

I had a year to plan. A year to learn and practice and write and practice more. Time flew by and before I knew it, it was time to write the one-hour presentation. After watching me struggle to write my presentation using my phone, Terry saved up some money and surprised me with a laptop. I typed away night after night and only got through part of the presentation when I looked at him and said, "I can't write it like this. It feels like I'm writing a book, not a speech."

That night we went to bed and I woke up at 3 a.m.

from a dream. I sat straight up after clearly hearing the words "write a book."

Terry woke up with me after I startled him awake, and before I could even tell him what I heard, he said, "I think you should do it, honey. Write a book."

So that's when I started to write what you are reading now. I pulled from the book's outline and used that to write the presentation for my first public speaking event. I then decided to kick off a public social media page where I could share stories, inspiration, and gather a group of people who want to grow. From those social media platforms came another idea to start a program called "GLOW", which stands for Growth, Love, Opportunity, and Worth—all of the things that I have been speaking about in this book and all of the terms that I feel best describe my journey thus far.

As I write this, I have also started to write a guided journal, online program, a coaching business and ultimately a weekend retreat.

Our music career is in full swing, keeping us extremely busy with live performances, radio and news interviews, and exciting new things like music videos and a possible small European tour in the works after a choreographer in France choreographed a dance to "Anymore", and we discovered that the song and the dance are both popular in a region in France not far from Switzerland.

Every day I work on expanding our reach as a band and as a brand from the time I open my eyes in bed until the time I can't keep them open anymore. Late in 2019 we founded our corporation, The Carter Company, (an event company) and we are beyond thrilled to see what will come to us in this coming decade.

Sometimes it's hard for me to believe that I am the same flesh, bones, heart, and soul I was twenty years ago. I remember that girl and look to her often, if only to remind myself just how far I have come. There are parts of her that will always be me. There are parts of her that have taught me lessons I never wanted to learn but am so grateful that I did. There are parts of me now that look back at her and sometimes long for a simpler life, one that isn't so public and busy. A life that allows me to stay home on weekends and drink real caffeinated coffee, a habit that was broken when the heart palpitations showed up.

But I know that if I went back to that girl, back to that life, then I wouldn't have the platform needed for me to be heard, and I have things still left to say.

Do you know what the word microphone stands for? It stands for an instrument that converts sound waves into electrical energy variations which may then be amplified, transmitted, or recorded.

Yes, it amplifies energy. It's no wonder I feel my whole self with a mic in my hand.

Someone once said that it's important to write out your experience so that it can become the survival guide for someone else. My hopes are that this book becomes someone's survival guide. A tool, a trick in your bag, a way to escape a bad relationship or situation or a hopeless mindset and come back out on the other side clutching my story and ready to write yours. I hope I've brought you joy, healing through laughter, and most importantly, hope, resilience, and strength. Through my experiences and stories, I hope you see how everything is mapped out for us. Each trial and error is connecting us to our true self in some way, and each experience is a lesson, propelling us forward and deeper into our authentic self and purpose.

I hope you listen to every song we release a little differently knowing that yes, I was born with the gift of being a songwriter but knowing even more what led up to finally having a song or two on the radio.

I hope we continue to learn together. This isn't a fiction book or movie like *Sweet Home Alabama* when Reese Witherspoon somehow avoids getting struck by lightning and marries her childhood sweetheart instead. If you have come to know me through this book, you know that I would have tripped over something during that storm on the beach and ended up being sued for slander for leaving the rich politician. Because this is real life. Not a movie.

In fact, I struggled for two months trying to figure out how to wrap it up and end the book. Partly because I needed a project to keep my mind off of things like turning forty-one and still fighting the feeling of having not "made it" in the music industry. Yet despite all of the amazing triumphs, an ongoing battle takes over me like a giant wave at times, forcing me to pull myself back up from the undertow and shake it off and get back to work. I am still trying to heal some huge gaping wounds that break open and bleed at the most random times, but I mostly struggled with how to end this book because how do you end a story that is still being written?

Every day I find I'm faced with a trial, a lesson, or a discovery that I want to dissect and navigate with you, and I never know where to end the book and save the rest for later. This is my main fuel for continuing my journey through podcasts and blogging. I still have a lot to say, and I hope you will still want to listen.

Thank you for allowing me to share my life with you through this book, through song, or through our interactions, be it online or in person. I see all of you and I love you all overwhelmingly. Without every single one of you, my story would be changed. You are all a part of what comes next now. You are all imprinted on my heart forever. You have read about the most vulnerable parts of me and the most private parts of my journey, so I hope that makes us connected in some way going forward.

The last message I want to leave you with is this: you are important in this world. What you have to give is so desperately needed. You were put here for a reason and without every spoke, the wheel doesn't turn. Love yourself a little today and show yourself some mercy. Forgive yourself for the moments you weren't thinking clearly and use that emotion inside of you to do good things. Help others. Be kind. Be gracious and never pass up a chance to have a hot cup of coffee with an old friend.

Life is short, my loves, and we are all just walking each other home. Leave your imprint on this world in the most positive and loving way you can, and promise me that you will never, ever give up. I love you.

XOJM

About the Author

Jonelle Marie Carter is a singer/songwriter, entrepreneur, blogger, author, and personal development coach hailing from the rural village of Seneca, Illinois.

She now resides in the Southwest suburbs of Chicago with her husband, musician, Terry Carter. Jonelle enjoys spending time with her children and two dogs, Bella and Willie.

Most nights, you can find her writing music, working on passion projects, performing with her acoustic band, River Road Trio, or dining with those closest to her.

Jonelle believes that everyone has a purpose and her passion is to help others discover their true potential while becoming an authentic and powerful version of themselves.

To follow along with Jonelle, visit her blog at www.jonellemariecarter.com

Acknowledgments

Thank you to

My parents Larry and Jo Ellen Fish for teaching me that anything is possible

My husband Terry Wayne Carter for showing me what unconditional love looks like

Our children- Shelby, Daniel, Travis and Marleyna

Mike Veny

Kate Tilton

Christie Stratos

Steve, Cody and Amy Rogers

Deborah and John Anthony

Glendon Haddix

To everyone who has encouraged me to tell my story & those who helped write it

www.ingramcontent.com/pod-product-compliance
Lightning Source LLC
Chambersburg PA
CBHW021521220426
43209CB00099B/1